Opposing Poetries

VOLUME I

Issues and Institutions

Opposing Poetries

VOLUME I

Issues and Institutions

HANK LAZER

Northwestern

University Press

Evanston

Illinois

Northwestern University Press
Evanston, Illinois 60208

Copyright © 1996 by Northwestern University Press
All rights reserved
Printed in the United States of America
ISBN 0-8101-1264-7 cloth
0-8101-1265-5 paper

Library of Congress Cataloging-in-Publication Data

Lazer, Hank.
Opposing poetries / Hank Lazer.
p.   cm. — (Avant-garde and modernism studies)
Includes bibliographical references (p.   ).
Contents: v. 1. Issues and institutions.   v. 2. Readings.
ISBN 0-8101-1264-7 (cloth : alk. paper : v. 1). —ISBN
0-8101-1265-5 (paper : alk. paper: v. 1). — ISBN 0-8101-1413-5 (cloth:
alk. paper : v. 2). — ISBN 0-8101-1414-3 (paper: alk. paper : v. 2).
1. American poetry—20th century—History and criticism—Theory,
etc.   2. Experimental poetry, American—History and criticism—
Theory, etc.   3. Modernism (Literature)—United States.   I. Title.
II. Series.
PS325.L39   1996
811'.5409—dc20   96-12315
                                                                                   CIP

FOR MARJORIE PERLOFF

Contents

Acknowledgments, ix

Introduction, 1

1   Criticism and the Crisis in American Poetry, 6

2   Opposing Poetry, 37

3   Poetry Readings and the Contemporary Canon, 47

4   The Politics of Form and Poetry's Other Subjects:

     Reading Contemporary American Poetry, 55

5   Experimentation and Politics:

     Contemporary Poetry as Commodity, 79

6   Thinking Made in the Mouth:

     The Cultural Politics of David Antin and Jerome Rothenberg, 91

7   Anthologies, Poetry, and Postmodernism, 126

Conclusion, 144

Notes, 153

Works Cited, 161

Index, 169

Acknowledgments

My thanks to many friends and students who, over the past ten years, listened to my ideas and shared with me their questions, perspectives, and observations on contemporary American poetry. Thanks also to James D. Yarbrough, dean of the College of Arts and Sciences at the University of Alabama, who supported my work on this book, and to Debbie St. John and William Martin for their dedicated work in preparing the final manuscript. And finally, special thanks to Marjorie Perloff, an articulate and energetic enthusiast on behalf of new poetries. *Opposing Poetries* is dedicated to this inspiring friend, colleague, and exemplar.

The chapters included here originally appeared, often in somewhat different form, in the following books and journals. My thanks to the editors of these journals for their encouragement and assistance.

"Criticism and the Crisis in American Poetry" appeared in the *Missouri Review* 9, no. 1 (1986).

"Opposing Poetry" appeared in *Contemporary Literature* 30 (Spring 1989).

"Poetry Readings and the Contemporary Canon" was originally delivered in a slightly different version at the 1988 MLA Convention and appeared in *American Poetry* 7, No. 2 (Winter 1990).

"The Politics of Form and Poetry's Other Subject: Reading Contemporary American Poetry" appeared in *American Literary History* 2, no. 3 (Fall 1990).

"Experimentation and Politics: Contemporary Poetry as Commodity" was originally delivered at the 1991 American Library Association convention and appeared in *Collection Management* 16, no. 4 (1992).

"Thinking Made in the Mouth: The Cultural Poetics of David Antin and Jerome Rothenberg" appeared in *Picturing Cultural Values* ed. William Doty, Tuscaloosa, University of Alabama Press, 1995.

"Anthologies, Poetry, and Postmodernism" appeared in *Contemporary Literature* 36, no. 2 (Summer 1995).

I am grateful to the authors and publishers listed below for the permission to reprint material quoted in *Opposing Poetries*.

Reprinted with permission of the author and the publisher passages from *Getting Ready to Have Been Frightened* by Bruce Andrews, New York: Roof Books, Copyright 1988.

Reprinted with permission of the author and the publisher phrases from "Swaps Ego," by Bruce Andrews in *Give Em Enough Rope* (Los Angeles: Sun & Moon Press, 1987), pages 84 & 114. Copyright 1987 by Bruce Andrews.

Passages from *Code of Flag Behavior* and *Meditations* by David Antin in *Selected Poems 1963–1973* (Los Angeles: Sun & Moon Press, 1991), pages 35–36, 39, and 143, Copyright 1991, 1971, 1968 by David Antin. Reprinted by permission of the publisher and the author.

Reprinted with permission of the author and publisher passages from *Talking at the Boundaries* by David Antin, New York: New Directions, Copyright 1976.

Reprinted with permission of the author and publisher passages from *Tuning* by David Antin, New York: New Directions, Copyright 1984.

Reprinted with permission of the author and publisher passages from *What It Means to be Avant-Garde* by David Antin, New York: New Directions, Copyright 1993.

Reprinted with permission of the publisher and the author passages from *A Poetics* by Charles Bernstein, Cambridge: Harvard University Press, Copyright 1992 by Charles Bernstein.

Reprinted with permission of the publisher and the author passages from *Controlling Interests* by Charles Bernstein, New York: Roof Books, Copyright 1980, 1986.

Passages from *Dark City* by Charles Bernstein, Los Angeles: Sun & Moon Press, 1994, pages 22–23, 51, 64, 81, 85, 105-6, 114, 139, 145–46. Copyright 1994 by Charles Bernstein. Reprinted by permission of the publisher and the author.

Passages from "You" in *Resistance* by Charles Bernstein, Windsor, VT.: Awede Press, 1983, Copyright 1983 by Charles Bernstein. Reprinted by permission of Sun & Moon Press and the author.

Reprinted with permission of the publisher passages from *Striking Resemblance* by Tina Darragh, Providence, R.I.: Burning Deck, Copyright 1989.

Reprinted with permission of the author and the publisher passages from *Tabula Rosa* by Rachel Blau DuPlessis, Elmwood, Conn.: Potes & Poets Press, Copyright 1987.

Reprinted with permission of the author and the publisher, phrases from *My Life* by Lyn Hejinian, Los Angeles, California: Sun & Moon Press, pages 25–26, Copyright 1980, 1987 by Lyn Hejinian.

Reprinted by permission of the author and the publisher passages from

Writing Is an Aid to Memory by Lyn Hejinian, The Figures, copyright 1978.

Susan Howe, excerpt from *Singularities*, pp. 49, Copyright 1990 by Susan Howe, Wesleyan University Press, reprinted by permission of the author and of University Press of New England.

Reprinted with permission of the author and the publisher, "The Wrong Can of Words" by Stuart Klawans, letter to the editor, October 3, 1988, in *The Nation*.

Passages from *Maxims from My Mother's Milk/Hymns to Him: A Dialogue* by Douglas Messerli, Los Angeles: Sun & Moon Press, 1988, pages 13, 17, 18, 43, Copyright 1988 by Douglas Messerli. Reprinted by permission of the publisher.

Reprinted with permission of the author, excerpt from *To the Reader* by Bob Perelman, Berkeley, California: Tuumba Press, Copyright 1984.

Reprinted with permission of the author and the publisher passages from *Errata 5uite* by Joan Retallack, Washington D.C.: Edge Books, Copyright 1993.

Reprinted with permission of the author and the publisher passages from *Lit* by Ron Silliman, Elmwood, Conn.: Potes & Poets Press, Copyright 1987.

"The House Was Quiet and the World Was Calm," from *Collected Poems* by Wallace Stevens, Copyright 1947 by Wallace Stevens. Reprinted by permission of Alfred A. Knopf.

Introduction

Opposing Poetries presents, in two volumes, a selection of nine years of writing on a range of issues in contemporary American poetry. These two volumes are not monological: I do not trace a single argument from beginning to end. I have left in the occasional nature of many of these essays and addresses, rather than manufacture expository transitions in the name of chapters pretending to belong to a unified book. As a reader of books on contemporary American poetry for university presses such as Harvard, Louisiana State, Alabama, and the State University of New York, and as a general reader of many more books on contemporary American poetry, I've been stuck by how often the best of such monological books is contained in their introductions, with the rest of the book being a far less interesting amassing of evidence and examples.

There are, of course, disadvantages to retaining the original format of these essays and addresses. There are overlaps and repetitions. Certain key quotations and key claims get repeated, though I hope in different enough contexts to be worth the shifting reconsiderations. If I were to write today on these same subjects, I would have different things to say. Of course, we all tend to imagine that with time we get wiser, more insightful, more intelligent, less inclined to naive enthusiasms. But that naive enthusiasm is also energizing and revelatory, and should not be erased. In the case of a number of these essays, I have restored previously deleted material and have attempted throughout to update references and publication information.

The essays in *Opposing Poetries* constitute a kind of temporal cubism, a slowly shifting but repeated focus on several key issues: the consequences of poetry's institutionalization; the pedagogical and political value of experimental poetry; and the crisis in self-representation (or the crisis that results from professionalized, mainstream poets' frequent misidentification of poetry with self-expression). Through a series of recurring cultural, material, and institutional perspectives, in *Opposing Poetries* I investigate assumptions and habits that govern conflicting conceptions of contemporary American poetry. In the course of the essays, I refine, reconsider, and question my own assertions and claims for experimental poetries.

While the Language poets are the principal group of poets I analyze, they constitute only a part of what I call "opposing poetries," that is, poetries that critique and contest assumptions and practices of more mainstream poetries. The term Language poetry itself is, in the course of this collection of essays, gradually questioned and understood to be a label or metonym that enables certain conversations and discussions, but the term itself actually comes to refer to a broader range of experimental poetries—including varieties of ethnopoetics, oral and performance poetries, and feminist poetries—many of which have at most a tangential relationship to the group of poets actually associated with $L=A=N=G=U=A=G=E$ magazine in the late 1970s and early 1980s.

I begin *Issues and Institutions*, the first volume of *Opposing Poetries*, with "Criticism and the Crisis in American Poetry," an examination of critical books in the mid-1980s that, in one way or another, attempt to theorize, historicize, or map contemporary American poetry from the 1960s to the mid-1980s. I focus on critical attempts to homogenize (through acts of exclusion) and institutionalize various versions of contemporary American poetry. In the essay I identify a series of conclusions about contemporary American poetry that stem from xenophobic reading habits. This essay is one of the very first substantial articles (along with a review by Michael Davidson in 1985 in the *New York Times Book Review* and a review-essay by Marjorie Perloff in 1986 in the *American Poetry Review*) in a mainstream literary journal to be devoted to a detailed consideration of the poetics of Language poetry and is the first published detailed reading of Charles Bernstein's *Content's Dream: Essays 1975–1984* (Bernstein 1986).

Chapter 1 thus presents several key premises for the entire collection. The first is that poetic practice is undergoing a significant shift in governing assumptions. That shift in attention—from the self to language—is part of what I investigate throughout *Issues and Institutions*. Chapter 1 also raises recurring questions for the entire collection: Where do we locate the political elements of poetry? What do we make of the fact that much contemporary poetry which claims the label "political" is presented in a conservative mode of writing and is allied with an authoritarian model of reading? Throughout this book, I consider ways of treating form, as well as reader-writer relationships, as of greater importance than message or content in determining the politics of a poem. The particular historical perspective that begins *Issues and Institutions* is that

> the poetic revolution of the late fifties and early sixties has ceased to invigorate the writing of poetry precisely at the moment when that poetic paradigm finds itself most thoroughly in control of official verse culture. This crisis is compounded by the fact that many poets and critics,

while aware of the predominantly dull product being turned out today, are either unaware of or choose to ignore the existence of a counter-poetics of real vitality. While American poetry may be alive and well, its institutionalized form is both terminally ill and well-entrenched, circumstances which make for a particularly painful and disputatious moment in our poetry. (Chapter 1)

Chapter 2, "Opposing Poetry," examines two groundbreaking anthologies, *"Language" Poetries* (Messerli 1987) and *In the American Tree* (Silliman 1986), and extends the analysis begun in Chapter 1 of the oppositional nature of Language poetry. In "Poetry Readings and the Contemporary Canon" (Chapter 3), I address the oral dimension of poetry and develop a statistical analysis of universities' support of various kinds of poetries through sponsorship of poetry readings. Indirectly, the support of various poets through poetry readings raises the broader issue of how public institutions such as universities and colleges are to respond to a newly decentralized (and more fragmented) world of poetry publication and distribution. This issue of the publication and distribution of poetry receives extended treatment in Chapter 5, "Experimentation and Politics: Contemporary Poetry as Commodity," where I focus on the purchase and approval plans of research libraries and their relationship to the diverse modes of poetry publication.

In "The Politics of Form and Poetry's Other Subjects: Reading Contemporary American Poetry" (Chapter 4), I examine a slightly different environment for the reading of contemporary poetry. Whereas the critical writings of the mid-1980s were characterized by a broad consensus that "something's wrong out there," the work of the late 1980s shows a series of different concerns. These later writings are much more receptive to a range of critical theory and to the importance of "otherness" in poetry. This body of criticism also demonstrates greater awareness of the many differences *within* contemporary American poetry. In this chapter I develop two topics central to an understanding of contemporary American poetry: "the dissemination of 'the subject,' accomplished variously by formal innovation, theoretical argument, and multicultural studies," and "the politics of poetry as a *resistance to appropriation*: resistance to the official verse culture, the marketplace, the dominant culture, and hegemonic ideologies."

In Chapter 4, I also begin to explore the pedagogical, political, and heuristic values of encounters with avant-garde writing. I propose that reactions to experimental writing involve fundamental habits of inclusion and exclusion and are crucial instances of treatment of the "other." Such tests of our tolerance of differing ways of making sense bear a close resemblance to issues of tolerance and difference in multiculturalism. However, in this essay I introduce a different perspective on the value of multiculturalism, proposing that education-by-difference must be considered fundamentally from a perspective of aesthetics and form (as well as subject matter). The particular danger I point out in much current espousal of multiculturalism is that often the poetry that is put forward as representative or "good" may in fact stem from a homogenized version of professionalized verse practice that merely reinforces outmoded versions of subjectivity and restricted modes of sense-making. Finally, I argue that definitions of "craft" and "quality" are always already ideological and are already implicated in cultural and institutional struggles.

"Thinking Made in the Mouth: The Cultural Poetics of David Antin and Jerome Rothenberg" (Chapter 6) involves a study of oral/performance poetry and ethnopoetics as critiques of the notion that poetry be defined by the personal lyric. In this essay I examine poetries that direct us toward sources and disciplines beyond what are conventionally considered to be literary and poetic, including anthropology, archaeology, linguistics, philosophy, and mythography. The work of Antin and Rothenberg demonstrates the value of a radical rethinking of the relationships between the modern and the (so-called) primitive. In the course of this chapter, several issues emerge that are central to the overall enterprise of *Opposing Poetries*: the need to develop an ongoing (rather than retrospective) view of modernism; the need to rethink possible locations and natures of "meaning" in poetry; and the role of poetry in unsettling the most widely held preconceptions in our culture.

In Chapter 7, "Anthologies, Poetry, and Postmodernism," I examine the ways in which three different anthology editors, Paul Lauter, Paul Hoover, and Douglas Messerli, conceptualize and represent American poetry of the latter half of the century. By analyzing the underlying assumptions for inclusion and exclusion for these three recent anthologies, I return to an issue raised in Chapter 4: the relationship between multiculturalism and formal innovation. While my main concern in this chapter is with conflicting compilations of innovation and the range of deviations from accepted patterns of literary representation, I also consider these anthologies as somewhat nostalgic artifacts produced near the end of a book-culture undergoing substantial change.

Thus, in this first volume, *Issues and Institutions*, I gather together essays and addresses that examine, for the most part, more broadly conceived theoretical and material issues regarding the recent reception and practice of poetry in the United States. (The second volume, *Readings*, presents, for the most part, essays focused on individual books of poetry and on the works and poetics of a range of individual writers.) In *Issues and Institutions*, I am especially concerned with institutional practices and locations. For the past fifteen years, my own praxis might be seen as interventionist in nature. I have attempted to write criticism and to publish it in places that might broaden, challenge, and redefine the kind of critical discussions of poetry that take place within the world of official verse culture. Thus, some of the writing in *Issues and Institutions* originally appeared in journals such as the *Missouri Review, Contemporary Literature, American Literary History*, and *Collection Management* (an important journal for university libraries); some writings in *Readings* were first printed in *The Nation*, the *Virginia Quarterly Review*, and the *American Poetry Review*. Such publications, and occasional talks at the American Library Association's annual convention, the Twentieth Century Literature Conference, and at the Modern Language Association continue work that I began with a symposium, "What Is a Poet?" held at the University of Alabama in October 1984. That event, which involved the participation of Charles Altieri, Charles Bernstein, Kenneth Burke, David Ignatow, Denise Levertov, Marjorie Perloff, Louis Simpson, Gerald Stern, and Helen Vendler, concluded with a lively panel discussion; the talks and the panel discussion were subsequently published (Lazer 1987).

Thus, *Opposing Poetries* continues my practice of a relatively lucid public advocacy of experimental poetries. For some readers, *Opposing Poetries* may provide an introduction to a range of innovative poetries; for others, it may extend, complicate, and inform an ongoing area of engagement.

Even with its wider pluralism, the early eighties has its own boundaries, though they will probably not be clear to us until they are challenged by some strongly innovative poets.

—James E. B. Breslin

Only in poetry do we find reflected Williams' image of Burr's dream — a democracy in permanent and celebratory revolution.

—Cary Nelson

1. Criticism and the Crisis in American Poetry

On October 18, 1984, Louis Simpson opened the Eleventh Alabama Symposium: What Is a Poet? with a talk entitled "The Character of the Poet." He began:

> For twenty years American poets have not discussed the nature of poetry. There has not been the exchange of ideas there used to be. The polemics of the Beat, the Black Mountain, the Sixties Poets, and the New York Poets are a thing of the past. The resistance to the war in Vietnam brought poets of different groups together on the same platform, and since that time they have ceased to argue—perhaps because arguing over poetry seems trivial when we are living under the shadow of nuclear annihilation. Another reason is the ascendancy of criticism. If poets do not speak for themselves others will speak for them, and when poets vacated the platform critics rushed to take their place. Those who have no great liking for poetry like to explain. The poets have been willing to see this happen—they believe that the best literary criticism and the only kind that's likely to last is a poem.[1]

After Simpson completed his address, a lively question and answer session developed. Among those who challenged Simpson were Marjorie Perloff, Charles Altieri, and Charles Bernstein, all of whom had recently written a great deal about contemporary poetry. I cite Simpson's remarks because he was both very right and very wrong. Simpson was correct about the winding down of the poetic and polemic projects spawned in the sixties. His generation of poets, the groundbreakers of the sixties who forged an alternative to the formal, ironic academic verse of the fifties, had, by the 1980s, become the literary establishment. Indeed, one of the major projects of criticism in the 1980s has been to offer an assessment and history of Simpson's generation.

While many of that generation turned away from the kind of critical writing that Simpson characterizes as "abstract thinking," to say that poets generally had vacated the platform and that serious, heated exchanges about the nature of poetry were a thing of the past is illustrative of the blindness or partialness that plagues the environment of contemporary American poetry. Reading books and essays of the 1980s by Charles Altieri, Ron Silliman, Stephen Fredman, Charles Bernstein, Marjorie Perloff, Bob Perelman, and Barrett Watten, I am led to wonder how such remarks about an end to argument could even be made, let alone become a commonly accepted attitude among readers and writers of contemporary poetry.

I find several projects (broadly characterized, and with considerable overlapping from category to category) being carried on in the essays and criticism of the early to mid-1980s: (1) evaluative or aesthetic criticism, with an emphasis on the appreciative (here, Randall Jarrell's descendants, after Richard Howard, are critics and poets such as Helen Vendler, Robert Hass, Peter Stitt, and Dave Smith); (2) thematic approaches to contemporary poetry (Alan Williamson and Cary Nelson); (3) the writing of traditional literary history for the poetry of the sixties and seventies (Jerome Mazzaro, James E. B. Breslin, and, with a radically different emphasis, Marjorie Perloff); and (4) an expression of "poetry in crisis" (Charles Altieri, Charles Bernstein, and Stephen Fredman) that involves several related issues: the impact of philosophy and critical theory on the reading and writing of poetry, a rereading of modernism as part of a program for innovation and renewal, and an assessment of the problems of the institutionalization (and attendant professionalization) of "being a poet." In this chapter, I shall examine at least one book from each category, but most of my attention finally will be devoted to the fourth area because, in my opinion, it is the flashpoint for critical discussions of poetry. So that my own writing does not become merely a carefully researched list of laments about what is lacking in contemporary poetry, I devote considerable attention to Charles Bernstein's essays; they challenge many commonly accepted views about style, ideology, reading, and our relationship to language and the production of meaning. Bernstein's work seems to me to be representative of the kind of serious thinking about poetry that has been ignored in most approaches of the mid-1980s to contemporary American poetry.

Symptomatic of the problem is Peter Stitt's *The World's Hieroglyphic Beauty* (1985), a series of essays followed by interviews with Richard Wilbur, William Stafford, Louis Simpson, James Wright, and Robert Penn Warren. Stitt claims that his book is primarily a thematic study:

> Generally speaking, what we see in the work of each of these writers is a quest through the physical world in search of an essence of meaning that is felt but never quite seen, desired but never quite defined. . . . The poets studied in this volume all love the physical world to such a degree that they sense within it some transcendent meaning, some hovering aura of belief. Roughly speaking, the quest each undertakes is to discover that hidden meaning by reading the "hieroglyphic" nature of the physical universe. (2)

As if the developments and complexities of literary criticism in the seventies and eighties had never taken place, Stitt proposes at the outset to write good old humanism, with sincerity and respect, and with its attendant hostility to "theory," its lack of interest in questions about the nature of language, or representation, and with a model of communication which supposes that "meaning" is some fixed commodity out there waiting to be relayed (whole?) to "the reader." I don't really fault Stitt for holding these views, which are close to those of Simpson and Smith, and the polar opposite of Charles Bernstein. What *does* distress me is that in 1985 Stitt would hold these views without reflection, without some serious self-questioning, and without considering the implications of such a view of poetry and language. Later in his book, when Stitt tries to characterize what he calls "that minority movement known as postmodernism," he mischaracterizes it by saying it is a "rather specialized approach to the possibilities of literature" where "the spirits of play and parody are preeminent and in which the poet's commitment is to the logic of the poem's world rather than to the external truth of the world that surrounds him" (69). For Stitt to convince us of the validity of his position, he needs to offer some consideration of the relationship between the poem (or words) and "the external truth of the world"—the latter, for me, being hard to imagine as existing *apart* from language.

While Stitt is out of his element in this more theoretical aspect of poetry, his writing does have some definite virtues. He does well as an appreciator of fine poetry; he has enough skepticism to be an excellent reviewer, as any reader of the *Georgia Review* of the 1970s and 1980s is well aware. While his reading of individual poems sticks too closely to mere description and paraphrase, he still does manage to produce especially fine essays on Simpson and James Wright (Stitt is Wright's authorized biographer); his research is thorough, and he is uncommonly good at conducting and editing interviews. Stitt asks good questions, eliciting interesting and revealing responses. With Simpson, for example, Stitt is aware that the interview is taking place during a transition in Simpson's poetic style, and gets Simpson to talk about the poetry he would like to write about "ordinary things" (144). Throughout the Simpson interview, we get a detailed statement of a theory of language's (potential) transparency that is the exact opposite of that proposed by Bernstein and others:

> I want to write an almost transparent poem in which you can't find the writer and in which the language draws no attention to itself. I know this attitude toward the language of poetry is completely different from that held by a poet like Dylan Thomas, back then, or today by a poet like Charles Wright, where the words are so important, or John Ashbery, where the individual sentences call so much attention to themselves. (148)

This debate over the transparency versus the materiality of the word is at the heart of emerging controversies in the mid-1980s, and Stitt's interview with Simpson does a great service by calling forth the "transparency" side of the argument. For me, the interviews—in less capable hands, a chatty, unfocused medium—are a major highlight of Stitt's book.

In these interviews we also get glimpses of the subject matter that I shall pursue throughout this chapter: the state of American poetry in 1985, its sources of controversy and crisis. William Stafford, surprisingly, voices a variety of discontent that will reappear in the work of Altieri, Breslin, and others. When asked which contemporary poets he most admires, Stafford replies:

> Mostly I like to read prose now. I think I prefer prose to poetry. I think there are more talented people writing prose than poetry in our country today. Besides, poetry is trapped trying to do little adventitious, piddling jobs, even today when it seems to be flourishing. It is interesting, but it isn't overwhelming the way Pascal is overwhelming, or the way some writer like Alfred North Whitehead, who turns his first-class mind to a sustained communication project, is overwhelming. I think

there are many prose projects now that are calling forth more the talents and the serious and sustained attention of writers than the kind of crochet work many of us are doing in poetry. (97)

Dave Smith, like Stafford, Donald Hall, and others, is concerned with the limitations of contemporary poetry. In *Local Assays: On Contemporary American Poetry* (1985), he portrays that smallness in large terms: "Too many poets lack the necessary intensity of speculation by which poetry moves the reader from sight to knowledge. Much of our poetry is aggressively trivial, as if it feared being thought overserious, righteous, or ambitious" (16). Smith finds among us "too many boring dreamers of little manner whose ambition is no more than a modest journalism" (32). If we ask what is to be done, Smith directs our attention to the nature of language and representation:

> Words are representational and chosen. They are not organic. . . . The word is a symbolic conventional sound. We live in time and convention. . . . We exist representationally, in that world of exchange, and to imagine we could do otherwise would be to resist, if not ignore, our shared heritage and meaning in history. (21)

Smith seems to regard his position as an embattled one, threatened on one flank by experimental writing and on the other by an overdecorous formalism: "We are at the threshold, if not already in the room, of a conservative poetics which threatens a new age of such versifiers and palace tutors. Two examples are John Hollander and William Harmon" (29). What remains praiseworthy for Smith is a narrow, but rich, plainspoken humanism:

> Responsible writing is accessible because it considers an audience, a communication, and accepts the duty to make referential exchange. The stream of bad books of poetry is thickened more by sloppy, inattentive, aesthetically liberated poets than by anything else. . . . If poetry is to exercise the powers of vision, prophecy, action, and beauty which poets still claim for their art, then poets need to make their poems more accessible through greater discipline, not liberation.
>
> Accessibility means also to suggest a poem of ordinary human experience enacted dramatically. Any poem must have some drama in it or the poem is divorced from life's energy. (5)

Smith is voicing the poetics of institutionalized poetry workshops, a poetics that Altieri will attack as "the scenic mode" and Bernstein as "official verse culture." Smith does *not* hide his position by pretending neutrality, open-mindedness, or "common sense." He argues for what he sees as a moral position, but it is also, at times, a narrowly moralistic poetics. He is prone to write about "the poet," "the life of the contemporary American poet," and what all poems should do. Perhaps expecting his own moral enthusiasm to carry us along, as in his argument for a "responsible" poetry, Smith is given to bombastic overstatement: "The function of poetry's music is to make us hear reality" (41).

Nevertheless, his essays and reviews of individual poets are insightful, especially those on Robert Penn Warren, Richard Hugo, and Louis Simpson, who fulfill many of Smith's hopes for poetry. But his poetics seems limited. Instead of a poetry of enactment, he argues that "every poem *comments on* human experience: that is the poem's function" (my emphasis, 8); instead of the reader as collaborator in the production of meaning, he has the reader taking dictation:

> It [rhythm] is drawn from the personality of the poem's maker, from the emotional blood-pulse of the heart. Once it is impressed in the poem, it tells the reader's heart how fast to beat, how he should pace himself through the dramatic experience. . . . He controls subject, poem, and reader. (12)

> We ask the reader to participate in our imaginative act but we control, by the score of the language, the limits and range of the participation. We do not attempt to hide what we mean. (18)

The resulting poetry is inseparable from the poet's desire to make a shapely, well-crafted, unified piece of writing, which, he assumes, mirrors a similarly ordered world. Smith wants to persuade us that such poetry is exclusive and pure: "Prose, that is, represents imperfection's tendency; poetry shows the tendency to seek purity of expression. That is why prose is inclusive and poetry is exclusive" (39). Finally, sounding like an Edgar Allan Poe of the 1980s, Smith tries to free poetry from its painful attachment to time and history: "Poems may exist in forms but poetry exists only in form, in the fused moment of language where we seem to behold the beauty and curve of life freed from the bondage of time, place, and effort" (89).

Like Randall Jarrell, Robert Hass, in *Twentieth Century Pleasures: Prose on Poetry* (1984), writes best when he savors a poem, or when he makes a witty, outrageous observation: "Control was a crucial word for most of the New Critics, who tended to write about emotion the way the older

Scott Fitzgerald wrote about alcohol" (147). What Hass values in James Wright—sensibility—we as readers value in Hass's essays. He writes a humorous and pleasing fusion of autobiography and criticism that is not self-indulgent, but illustrative of how we read and locate poetry within the context of the rest of our lives. He excels at articulating his changing readings of a given poem or poet over time—a devotion based on a tenacity that few critics can match. Hass gives us the feeling that he lives with poetry, with those poems that truly matter to him, for quite some time *before* he begins to write an essay. The resulting essays are remarkable for their range of appeal. For example, his "Looking for Rilke," with its insightful reappraisal of the Orpheus myth, makes fine reading either for the reader unfamiliar with Rilke or for the already initiated. His essays on James Wright, Tomas Tranströmer, Czeslaw Milosz, and Rilke are each models of passion, lucidity, and, occasionally, skepticism. He writes a highly readable, even exciting, criticism, all the while articulating his own enthusiasm, carrying us along with him as he works out his own salvation as a poet. Hass's enthusiasms are contagious; with this first collection of essays, I am tempted to say that he has written a California sensualist's version of *The Pleasure of the Text* (Barthes 1975), whose principal critical project is to find a satisfactory vocabulary of praise.

The sense of crisis in contemporary American poetry that I shall be tracing in this chapter remains muted in Hass's book: "Now, I think, free verse has lost its edge, become neutral, the given instrument" (70). By casting his remarks primarily in the past tense, Hass does suggest that we stand at the end of a poetic era, one that has, to a large degree, been obsessed with the image: "Almost all the talk about poetry in the past few years has focused on issues of image and diction. There was a liveliness in the idea of hauling deep and surreal imagery into American poetry, but the deep image is no more structural than imagism: there was hardly any sense of what the rhythmic ground might be" (132). I think Hass sees the current task in poetry to be solving "the problem of getting from image to discourse in the language of his time" (148), but his own efforts flounder on a kind of hot-tub materialism. Discussing poems by Basho and Buson, Hass explains:

> What makes it a poem is the way it renders the sensation of having an idea, the slightly comic feeling that the thought itself is the sudden vacuum and after-whiff of lightning; so that, while the poem seems to be about seeing lightning without preconception, it is much more about

being lightning, or being struck by the lightning of thought. It is in this sense that the image stands for itself. It is a moment of insight that is a figure for a moment of insight, and this is why Buson's poem seems to keep expanding past its metaphorical targets, past art, past tools, past coolness and summer, until it seems to be not about but equal in status with being and the mysteriousness of being. (286)

With his own focus on sensation, incarnation, and poetic rendering, Hass builds a kind of mystical roadblock that prevents sustained thinking about poetry. By turning his attention to sensation itself, Hass prepares the way for his retreat from any serious consideration of the complexities of language and representation.

Perhaps because of his own ascendancy as a poet, or perhaps under the tutelage of Czeslaw Milosz, Hass also manages to ignore (or remain indifferent to) the varieties of poetic experimentation taking place all around him in the Bay Area. While his book, through well-wrought appreciations, does provide evidence for Pound's dictum "what thou lovest well remains," Hass's collection of essays does not really take the pulse of current poetry nor of current critical thinking. *Twentieth-Century Pleasures* remains rather conservative conceptually: close readings, appreciations (often rooted in autobiography), and extended prosodic analyses.

Like nearly all of the poets and critics I am considering, Alan Williamson in *Introspection and Contemporary Poetry* (1984) takes a principally thematic approach to the subject. Williamson also agrees that there is "something wrong" with much of today's poetry: "Over the last ten years, one has more of a sense of a single period style dominating the work of emerging poets than at any time since the 1950s. Or perhaps it is just that this period style, like the post-New Critical style of thirty years ago, seems a particularly disturbing one, in the range of intellectual and emotional experiences it excludes" (93). Williamson analyzes this crisis in cultural terms, referring to the writing of Christopher Lasch to support his view that if "the dominant emotional malaise of our time is a narcissism whose hallmark is not that it finds the self exciting, but that it never finds anything beyond the self exciting enough, then surely this is the poetry of that narcissism" (95). When he discusses the failings of contemporary poetry, Williamson correctly calls attention to Robert Pinsky's *The Situation of Poetry* (1976) as the book that began the critique of poetry's dominant mode in the seventies. But Williamson's antidote is increased attention to "the specific flavor of the poet's personality" (103), and his book becomes a defense of an approved list of poets whose work intensifies the acts of self-scrutiny and self-presentation. In spite of the possible dangers of narcissism that threaten such poetry, Williamson argues that "we also live with and through the self, as long as we live," and that "I see no need to apologize for rewarding the self as one of the great human and poetic subjects; always acknowledging that the most adequate poetry of the self is likely to be the most aware of its paradoxes, the least inclined to freeze it by abstracting it from the totality of its relations" (6). Williamson seeks the "transcendence of human isolation" through a poetry in which the poet becomes "at once the subject, for the reader, and object, for himself" (13).

While Williamson writes surprisingly well about Gregory Orr, and less surprisingly but equally well about Sylvia Plath, John Ashbery, Frank Bidart, and James McMichael, his book has serious flaws. It pretends to a larger thematic organization, but reads like a patchwork of essays and reviews that the author has not bothered to rewrite and rethink sufficiently; it remains too narrowly the work of a Robert Lowell disciple trying to please his literary papa. The "good," for Williamson, obsessively centers on personality, neurosis, and psychological tension, and thus he promotes a considerably diminished concept of poetry.

When, at the very end of his book, Williamson notes that "we reflect that perhaps, after all, all roads are always open in literature; it is only a question of the writer who knows how to travel them" (191), he ignores the fact that his own critical standards pave a superhighway for the poetry of self and personality while also creating serious roadblocks for other kinds of poetry. He criticizes a variety of experimental writing for avoiding "the traditional tests of high art" (106). Creeley's middle-period poems, the work of "younger members of the New York School such as Ted Berrigan," and others are attacked for their "jaded, exhausted tone," their "sense of a passive or empty 'I,'" their mistrust of significance itself, and their "incitation to literary mediocrity" (107). How, then, does John Ashbery's poetry gain favorable and insightful attention from Williamson? In part, because he finds plenty of psychological tension in Ashbery's work which, for Williamson, gives Ashbery's poetry "a force far exceeding mere aesthetic novelty" (122). But I also attribute that favorable attention to a more widespread practice in contemporary academic criticism—the domestication and acceptance of John Ashbery's experimental poetry as a kind of strategic tokenism. The academic subindustry devoted to Ashbery's work becomes a way both of acknowledging the value of experimental writing and a way of avoiding consideration of many other experiments in poetry. Ashbery's work cannot represent the full range of experimental writing, and an argument could be made for an increasingly quaint traditionalism to his work, with its Tennysonian, late-Victorian tone of wistfulness about time, mortality, and change.

One of the best of the mid-1980s historical approaches to contemporary poetry is James E. B. Breslin's *From Modern to Contemporary: American Poetry, 1945–1965* (1984). The finest chapters in the book are those devoted to James Wright, Frank O'Hara, and Allen Ginsberg. A careful researcher, particularly in a chapter on Ginsberg in which he makes extensive use of passages from the notebooks, Breslin choose a "historically informed formalist criticism" to present a detailed history of the poetic revolution of the late fifties and sixties:

> In these years the paradigms for poetry were transformed in ways that affected and still affect a whole generation of American poets. If now, some twenty years later, the insurgents of 1960 are comfortably occupying the literary armchairs and if their poetic procedures are beginning to look a little too easy, stiff, and predictable to younger poets, then the time may be right to go back and take an historical look at this originating moment in contemporary poetry. My own belief is that this moment saw the emergence of an antiformalist revolt which can best be understood by an historically informed formalist criticism — that is, one concerned with the changing theories and practices of poetic form. (xiv)

Breslin gains credence by recognizing that the revolt he traces is an established, institutionalized one, itself about to be overturned; he establishes a convincing picture of the narrowed, domesticated version of modernism that led to the revolt; his sense of periodization shows sophistication and good sense; and he knows the value of anecdote in the making of a lively, readable history. For example, the ghost of Eliot, the chief father of 1950s academic modernism, is relayed to us by an anecdote:

> It is perhaps an even more striking measure of Eliot's influence at the time that when he began "Howl," the poem that would do so much to dramatize the shift away from Eliot, Allen Ginsberg had a dream in which he appeared at a cocktail party at Eliot's London flat where his host at first naps in a farther room, but then comes forth to ask to read

Ginsberg's work, and Ginsberg weeps in gratitude for the recognition. One imagines that many of the best minds of Ginsberg's generation had *that* dream. (15)

I also admire Breslin's skepticism about periodization: "The whole sense of history as a dynamic *process* is lost by dichotomizing twentieth-century poetry into two static periods" (57). Breslin's readings in critical theory enhance his book; he absorbs certain crucial assumptions (from Foucault, Barthes, and others), but does not become trapped in cumbersome jargon: "Only by refusing the idea of a literary period as a stable unity can we account for change from one such era to the next" (62).

Breslin's book proves most exciting in its implied relationship between the climate of poetry in 1985 and that of the period following World War II: "when a young contemporary writer recalls, say, the ten years between the end of the Second World War and the mid-fifties, he or she is much more apt to imagine a crowded and stultifying space, one filled with the most suffocating presences of all—canonized revolutionaries" (1–2). He cites W. D. Snodgrass's statement that the "originally revolutionary movement had become something fixed, domineering and oppressive" (3), making today's situation, in the words of Yogi Berra, "seem like déjà vu all over again." Indeed, in his final chapter, "Our Town: Poetry and Criticism in the Early Eighties," Breslin makes explicit the parallels that have been implicit throughout his historical description:

> If American poetry in the middle fifties resembled a peaceful public park on a pleasant summer Sunday afternoon, and if by the early sixties it had been transformed into a war zone, the air heavy with manifestos, then by the early 1980s the atmosphere has lightened and the scene more resembles a small affluent town in Northern California. . . .
>
> No one seems moved by overweaning ambition or any desire to unsettle the way things are. . . . The town's politics are liberal—which means that while there is some gossip, some backbiting, and a few ancient and bitter feuds, there are no ideological disputes. . . .
>
> The rebels of 1960, in short, have now achieved prestige and authority. . . . As teachers, these poets conduct poetry workshops which, in the absence of any contemporary handbook or manual of poetics, have become powerful institutions in the last twenty years, with older poets here possessing the power to admit to writing programs and particular classes, to define quality, to provide literary and practical help,

and, in the awarding of degrees, to certify those members of the next generation who will teach writing. (250–51)

How does such a vision of stagnant harmony (in the present) come to be accepted, especially when Breslin and others posit continuous strife and eruptions as a persuasive model for literary history? Certainly Breslin's view of modernism and modernity is anything but static: "modernity can only be true to itself by continually denying itself; modernity is a radical enterprise, a perpetual crisis" (10). On the one hand, Breslin astutely observes that "the fifties' domestication of modernism thus ironically recreated exactly the kind of literary predicament that had prompted modernity in the first place and so legitimatized a new opening, a new revolt" (53). Yet, when Breslin offers a reading of the current climate, he seems slightly befuddled and unwilling (or unable) to locate the serious challenges to today's establishment:

> My characterization of the contemporary scene so far may suggest that poetry has come full circle and returned to the timidity of the early fifties. Certainly, the scarcity of risky innovation and demolition work, the preference for consolidation and generational continuity, plus the development of these trends within a reactionary political climate—all these establish striking parallels. (225)

The alternatives to a placid generational continuity that Breslin mentions are practically dismissed in the very act of naming them:

> The groundbreaking poets of two decades ago, however, have now settled in; they preside over a literary scene that shows plenty of life but few signs of avant-garde activity, except for the "language poets" and isolated figures like David Antin and John Cage. Donald Allen's New American Poetry is now almost twenty-five years old; . . . but no revolutionary anthology has risen to challenge, much less supersede it. (252)

Such bemoaning of the impoverished, stagnant state of contemporary poetry, we will see, is repeated in Charles Altieri's Self and Sensibility in Contemporary American Poetry (1984). But such a viewpoint is possible only through either an innocent or willed institutionalized xenophobia that arises from the reading habits of most academically based poets and critics. While they may know the history of modernism, they nevertheless insist on reading almost exclusively the poetry and criticism published by "major" commercial presses and a few university presses. Their reading habits actually seem to mirror the predominating narrowness and "exclusiveness" of the periods they so carefully chronicle. I am not complaining because one of my favorite writers has been ignored. In fact, many of my favorites—James Wright, John Ashbery, and Louis Simpson—have fared quite well. Academics, as a group—including the many poets who are institutionally based—have been content to debate the merits of John Ashbery's work as a substitute for considering a much broader, livelier, challenging spectrum of experimentation and revolt occurring in alternative presses.[2]

Even a passing glance at some of this material would make it impossible to lament, as Breslin does, "the disjunction between critical theory and poetic practice" (262). Outside the mainstream it is common to engage in both "theoretical" and "poetic" writing. Indeed, the two activities often overlap; they are seen as mutually reinforcing processes of thought and writing. Ours *is* a lively age, an age of strife, controversy, and, in a very specific sense, crisis. But the writing that would challenge the generational continuity and "canonized revolution" that Altieri and Breslin bemoan has been systematically ignored for a period of ten years by these very critics, the arbiters of what Bernstein calls "official verse culture."

Approaching today's American poetry, as I am, by way of a series of critical observations, the following descriptive remark by Paul de Man (1983) becomes particularly helpful:

> In periods that are not periods of crisis, or in individuals bent on avoiding crisis at all cost, there can be all kinds of approaches to literature: historical, philological, psychological, etc., but there can be no criticism. For such periods or individuals will never put the act of writing into question by relating to its specific intent. The Continental criticism of today is doing just that, and it therefore deserves to be called genuine literary criticism. It will become clear, I hope, that this is not to be considered as an evaluative but as a purely descriptive statement. Whether authentic criticism is a liability or an asset to literary studies as a whole remains an open question. One thing, however, is certain; namely, that literary studies cannot possibly refuse to take cognizance of its existence. It would be as if historians refused to acknowledge the existence of wars because they threaten to interfere with the serenity that is indispensable to an orderly pursuit of their discipline. (8)

Precisely because Altieri (1984) puts "the act of writing into question by relating to its specific intent," it offers, despite other shortcomings, the best-focused discussion of the mid-1980s crisis in contemporary American poetry.

When compared to the more common, craft-oriented, aesthetic criticism, Altieri's unwavering assumptions are refreshing: that "poems and arguments express cultural tensions" (5) and that we do best by "reading works as participants in a social drama" (6). In the manner of Kenneth Burke, Altieri believes that "poets become actors within a culture" (7). If Altieri's book did nothing else, its insistence upon locating poetic activity within a cultural and sociopolitical context makes it a valuable corrective to narrowly thematic and aesthetic approaches. Altieri argues

> that criticism of contemporary poetry ignores some of its basic responsibilities if it rests content with describing the work of individual poets. We fail our culture and we fail the poets if we do not seek some general contrastive basis on which to establish the significant tasks some poets must perform. Without a sense of the challenge poets face it is impossible to use more than aesthetic criteria in judging their work. (191)

Altieri's method is to study and explore the stylistic choices that connect poets to their culture. He describes the dominant poem of our times as "the scenic mode" and argues: "We most clearly see abstract analogues between the scenic mode and the essentially narcissistic upper-middle-class intellectuals if we attend to popular modes of self-presentation. Dramatic structures in the scenic mode beautifully reflect the dualities of the 'laid-back' style" (22). Altieri begins by being "suspicious about the values claimed for the ethos of naturalness" (15), and proceeds to zero in on the dishonesty inherent in the contemporary "sincere" poem's relationship to its own rhetorical methods: "The sincere self has no theater on which to stage itself except the theater it constructs. But such construction is pure rhetoric, the traditional opposite of sincerity, because the individual acts of self-staging shape what is made to appear natural" (23). Altieri's book is open to criticisms—his argument is often repetitive; his praise of Adrienne Rich is utterly unconvincing; he picks easy negative targets and relies too heavily on them to prove his case; and his sociopolitical arguments are sometimes fuzzy—but his critique of "the scenic mode" is accurate and essential to an understanding of the limitations of contemporary poetry.

While in the past (Lazer 1984) I have argued against the premises of Altieri's complaints, I find myself more and more won over to his view. Following up on Jonathan Holden's descriptions of the dominant mode in 1980s poetry, Altieri offers this description of a prevailing poetic paradigm:

A typical contemporary litany is easy to reproduce: Craft must be made unobtrusive so that the work appears spoken in a natural voice; there must be a sense of urgency and immediacy to this "affected natural-ness" so as to make it appear that one is reexperiencing the original event; there must be a "studied artlessness" that gives a sense of sponta-neous personal sincerity; and there must be a strong movement toward emphatic closure, a movement carried on primarily by the poet's ma-nipulation of narrative structure. (10)

Then, Altieri extends his description to include a characterization of speaker and tone, as well as what this paradigm excludes:

The work places a reticent, plain-speaking, and self-reflective speaker within a narratively presented scene evoking a sense of loss. Then the poet tries to resolve the loss in a moment of emotional poignance or wry acceptance that renders the entire lyric event an evocative meta-phor for some general sense of mystery about the human condition. . . . [T]he poems must clearly illustrate the controlling hand of the crafts-man, but the craft must remain subtle and unobtrusive. So the formal burden lies primarily on elaborate vowel and consonant music. The central aim of the art is not to interpret experience but to extend lan-guage to its limits in order to establish poignant awareness of what lies beyond words. There is virtually never any sustained act of formal, dia-lectical thinking, or any elaborate, artificial construction that cannot be imagined as taking place in, or at least extending from, settings in natu-ralistically conceived scenes. (10–11)

Admittedly, it is not damning in and of itself to be able to describe accu-rately the poetic conventions of a particular age. Any literary movement, whether conservative or avant-garde or something else, will be describable in terms of certain habits and assumptions. But Altieri makes us face the limitations of a particularly popular model, which I think of as comprising the ossified and institutionalized poetic conventions of the revolt of the late 1950s and early 1960s:

we have paid an enormous price for our poets' commitments to the expressive norm of sincerity and the thematic ideal of articulating a silence beyond cultural frameworks. In seeking absolutes, they cease to address one another or to take responsibility for making and testing contrastive languages. I think this is why we find almost all the instru-ments agreeing that ours is an age without much strong poetry. There are voices we sympathize with, but few presences we take into account when we elaborate our own contrastive frameworks for judging experience. (200–201)

Altieri believes that the lack of ambition, self-consciousness, and serious thought in the poems produced by the cult of sincerity explains "why poetry now fails to play any formative role in our culture" (203). Thus, Altieri may be right to suggest that "speculative criticism now attracts much of the audience and the energy the last decade devoted to poetry" (27).

From a similar perspective, Donald Hall (1983) writes about the McPoem, which he calls "the product of the workshops of Hamburger University" (95). Such poems, according to Hall, "are often *readable*, charming, funny, touching, sometimes even intelligent. But they are usually brief, they resemble each other, they are anecdotal, they do not extend themselves, they make no great claims, they connect small things to other small things" (91). Hall's critique points out how often impatience and an absence of ambition are essential to the workshop's methodology, suggesting that the university workshops merely provide "technology for mass reproduction of a model created elsewhere" (95).

Altieri is also critical of the institutional setting for poetry in his analysis of our current situation. He worries that writing workshops "reinforce and reproduce the guidebook mentality prevalent in our culture" (206). Like Hall, Altieri sees "the workshop as a material expression of the condition of production and consumption basic to our poetic culture" (206). Every bit as hazardous as the workshop's model of quick production and quick consumption, is the inevitable standardization of expectations through overattention to "craft":

> These workshops and the mentality they encourage put poets in a situation closely parallel to that of French painting in the 1850s. There, too, extraordinarily skillful artists created a climate skeptical of any intellectual role for the medium, hence trapping it within a narrow equation of lucidity with elegantly controlled surfaces. Instead of a stress on ideas, there emerged an emphasis on craft that in turn produced a highly inbred professionalism governing both the training of artists and the judgment of their work. (205)

What Altieri looks for is greater play, experimentation with form, a greater range of possible voices, a degree of skepticism and self-questioning

—in other words, a break with the now all-too-predictable, manipulative gestures of the "sincere" poem that "concentrate emotions instead of encouraging a lyric dialogue among competing voices in the self or among ideas the self tries out as interpretations of its experiences" (16). That is, poets must be willing to challenge the habits of craft, rhetoric, and gesture that currently make the lyric a diminished thing: "Poets will have to reflect on what their work is a reflection of, and they will probably have to combine the intensity of self-presentation with the lucidity of dramatic self-criticism" (205). I agree that without such rigorous and often disturbing self-reflection and self-criticism, poetry's relationship to our culture and our intellectual life will remain marginal. I would add that those poets who think the "sincere" mode is renovated by garnishing poems with a few weightier words—"history," "the mind," "language"—have not responded deeply enough to the problem and remain trapped within the narrow craft of a received, institutionalized poetic tradition that, by now, sacrifices more than it can include.

However, along with my admiration for Altieri's book, I do find that, again, much of his criticism of the diminished state of contemporary American poetry is made possible, perhaps even guaranteed, by his own narrow reading habits. As with Simpson's characterization of our poetic climate or Breslin's description of "our town," much of what Altieri wishes were taking place in poetry—reflections on rhetorical strategies, self-consciousness, experimentation, theoretical and intellectual depth, and so on—*is* out there, but not to be found within the narrowly circumscribed reading habits of most academically based poets and critics (Altieri, lamentably, included). Either innocently or willfully, he does not read the fairly extensive body of poetry and essays that would contradict his depiction of poetry's dominant mode. Academic poets (rather than critics) guilty of the same xenophobia are easier to understand. Clearly, the academic poets' xenophobia has to do with turf and the narrow professionalization of the creative writing industry.

One writer whose work would, if read, kick up a ruckus in the placid poetry-town described by Altieri, Breslin, Simpson, and others is Charles Bernstein, the author of ten books of poetry.[3] His *Content's Dream: Essays, 1975–1984* (1986) is the most exciting and challenging book of essays I have read in quite some time. The style, range of reference, and thought makes for stimulating reading, the kind that inevitably leads to other reading (as well as rereading). Bernstein includes analyses of film, philosophy (particularly the writings of Wittgenstein and Cavell, and a partial refutation of Derrida's work), the visual and plastic arts (with special attention to the work of Arakawa), rereadings of modernism (with particular attention to Gertrude Stein, William Carlos Williams, and Laura [Riding] Jackson), and plenty of reviews of neglected contemporary poets (including Ron Silliman, Jackson Mac Low, Lyn Hejinian, Robert Creeley, Robin Blaser, Ray Di Palma, Clark Coolidge, and Hannah Weiner), as well as providing an ideological framework for approaching poetry. Bernstein's writing is, like Thoreau's, both refreshing and accusatory. He practices a Kierkegaardian irony in his rigorous questioning of assumed content. Three particular essays—"Thought's Measure," "Writing and Method," and "The Academy in Peril: William Carlos Williams Meets the MLA"—merit detailed attention, in part for the contrast they provide to the academic community's token acceptance of Ashbery's work. I hope the following detailed exploration of Bernstein's essays encourages readings of other experimental writers; a similar exploration of Barrett Watten's *Total Syntax* (1985) or Ron Silliman's *The New Sentence* (1987) would just as effectively refute the characterization of contemporary poetry as a tranquil community free of serious argument.

To a certain extent, Bernstein's descriptions of the current situation in poetry resemble Altieri's. In his essay on Williams, Bernstein contends that "what characterizes the officially sanctioned verse of our time, no less than Williams', is a restricted vocabulary, neutral and univocal tone in the guise of voice or persona, grammar-book syntax, received conceits, static and unitary form. In Williams' terms, writing like this is *used* to convey emotions or ideas rather than allowed to enact them" (245). Bernstein sees many poets today cutting themselves off from the full range of writing because they "put themselves above theory or cultivate an ignorance of it and of the methodological implications of their craft, while projecting a picture of critical thinking as monolithic and anti-imaginative" (381). His attack on a diminished conception of poetry in our time explicitly includes Altieri's complaint about the unacknowledged rhetorical status of the "sincere" poem, but Bernstein extends that analysis by drawing out the philosophical and ideological implications of such a writing practice:

The "antirationalist" manifestation takes "thought" as "prohibiting emotion," as if they were two discrete objects trying to occupy the same space. But the *heroics* of personality, or the *everydayness* of everyday voice or thought, only disguises the intellectuality of the medium through which these things are expressed. It is this disguising, and not the expressions, that is the problem. . . .

The question is always: what is the meaning of this language practice; what value does it propagate; to what degree does it encourage an understanding, a visibility of its own values or to what degree does it repress that awareness? To what degree is it in dialogue with the reader and to what degree does it command or hypnotize the reader? Is its social function liberating or repressive? Such questions of course open up into much larger issues than ones of aesthetics, open the door by which aesthetics and ethics are unified. (157, 224–25)

In his effort to unify aesthetics and ethics, Bernstein makes his major contribution to discussions of contemporary poetry. He denies the commonly mistaken notion that experimentation is esoteric and therefore elitist, by focusing on style and form as the site for political activity. Not the message itself, but the imagined relationship between reader and writer and the ways in which meaning gets produced provide the essential location for the poem's ideological enactment.

Bernstein's claim is that so-called natural- or plain-style poetry hypnotizes its reader by discouraging or repressing any awareness of its own artifice and intellectuality, and that we find a different notion of reader and reading in the poetry of writers such as Jackson Mac Low, Ron Silliman, Lyn Hejinian, Bernstein himself, Hannah Weiner (and, to a lesser degree, poets such as Robert Creeley and John Ashbery), especially as these writers make certain that the *construction* of their work is *not* disguised. But a more ideologically desirable relationship to artifice (that is, to making, and thus to poesis itself) is not the only difference proposed by Bernstein: "To try to unify the style of work around this notion of self is to take the writing to be not only reductively autobiographical in trying to define the *sound* of me but also to accept that the creation of a persona is somehow central to writing poetry" (407). To put it quite succinctly, Bernstein says, "It's a mistake, I think, to posit the self as the primary organizing feature of writing" (408).

Such a critique, which is so at odds with many current views and practices of poetry, would seem to sweep away much of what interests writers such as Williamson and even Altieri, whose book, after all, is about "self and sensibility." For Bernstein, an alternative to an investigation of "self"—how the self is constituted and how it re-presents itself—is sustained attention to language and its operations: "The question that always interested me was how could language be made more conscious of itself, a question of the making audible of knowledge otherwise unreflected or unconscious. This making audible being the music of the poem" (407). In so doing, Bernstein again and again calls our attention to the ways in which we use language (which I see as precisely the "self-consciousness" or scrutiny that Altieri misses in much current poetry and criticism):

> The distortion is to imagine that knowledge has an "object" outside of the "language games" of which it is a part. . . . Indeed, the truth of skepticism is that there is meaning only "inside" our conventions, that it makes no sense to speak of meaning outside these contexts. (171, 173)

Which means that for Bernstein, "the order of the elements of a discourse is value constituting and indeed experience engendering, and therefore always at issue, never assumable" (221). Bernstein's understanding of language patterns as "value constituting" and "experience engendering" can lead to the plain stylist's nightmare: endless experimentation with form and style (as in Bernstein's own *Islets/Irritations* (1983) or much of Mac Low's writing); but it also leads to a more active role for reader and writer as co-producers of meaning and (now conscious) users of the medium through which meaning is produced: language.

Thus far, with a few notable exceptions, university-based poets and critics have practiced either benign neglect or an uninformed (and defensive) dismissal of a broad range of experimental writing because it's not emotionally moving, not interesting, just theory or structuralism, artificial, unreadable, not clear, too abstract, not making sense, all form or style and no content, self-indulgent, undisciplined, and so forth. In phrases remarkably similar to those used in reaction to John Ashbery's poetry twenty years ago, we are hearing the usual litany of attacks on "the new." As Paul de Man (1983) reminded us:

> Even in its most naive form, that of speculation, the critical act is concerned with conformity to origin or specificity: when we say of art that it is good or bad, we are in fact judging a certain degree of conformity to an original intent called artistic. We imply that bad art is barely art at all; good art, on the contrary, comes close to our preconceived and implicit notion of what art ought to be. (8)

As I have already suggested, there are, as always, motives of power, ideology, and economic self-interest behind such negative judgments. But, if I am correct about a state of crisis, such remarks are to be expected when artistic practice undergoes a radical shift in governing assumptions.

That shift in attention—from the self to language—is most fully explored in "Thought's Measure," which Bernstein (1986) begins with the following axiomatic remarks:

> Language is the material of both thinking and writing. We think and write in language, which sets up an intrinsic connection between the two.

> Just as language is not something that is separable from the world, but rather is the means by which the world is constituted, so thinking cannot be said to "accompany" the experiencing of the world in that it informs that experiencing. It is through language that we experience the world, indeed through language that meaning comes into the world and into being. As persons, we are born into language and world; they exist before us and after us. Our learning language is learning the terms by which a world gets seen. Language is the means of our socialization, our means of initiation into a (our) culture. I do not suggest that there is nothing beyond, or outside of, human language, but that there is meaning only in terms of language, that the givenness of language is the givenness of the world. (61–62)

Bernstein's argument in "Thought's Measure" deepens the relationship between form and content, making content a product of form and the concept of a *separate* entity called "content" merely a dream. Thus, new ways of writing become crucial to Bernstein precisely because "various shapes and modes and syntaxes create not alternate paraphrases of the same things but different entities entirely" (68). The excitement of such work as Ron Silliman's *Tjanting* (1981) or *Ketjak* (1978), David Antin's *Tuning* (1984), or Charles Bernstein's *Controlling Interests* (1980) or *Islets/Irritations* (1983) no longer resides in the "naturalistic" rendering of "sincere," powerful emotions nor moments of, by now, rather predictable "illumination." Instead, Bernstein wishes

> to make language opaque so that writing becomes more and more conscious of itself as world generating, object generating. This goes not only for making palpable the processes of the mind and heart (inseparable) but for revealing the form and structure in which writing occurs, the plasticity of form/shape. So that writing may be an experience in

which the forms and objects of the world may seem to be coming into being. (71)

Two particular consequences of Bernstein's rethinking of poetry are that "poetry need not privilege a particular kind of language as poetic" (310) and "as against other writing practices, poetry explicitly holds open the possibility of producing, rather than reproducing, ideas" (368), the latter notion continuing the very activity advocated and practiced by Gertrude Stein, William Carlos Williams (see especially W. C. Williams 1974), and others. For Bernstein, reading becomes a collaborative act where

> the text calls upon the reader to be actively involved in the process of constituting its meaning, the reader becoming a neutral observer neither to a described exteriority nor to an enacted interiority. The text formally involves the process of response/interpretation and in so doing makes the reader aware of herself or himself as producer as well as consumer of meaning. (233)

To state the obvious, such collaborative reading, the opposite of Smith's writer who dictates to his reader, involves an ideological model of text, reader, production, and consumption quite different from today's poetry of the dominant mode. For Bernstein, "this concept of reading extends beyond the text into the world, into the realm of reading human culture, furthering the activity of critique in Marx and interpretation in Freud" (236).

Bernstein, drawing heavily on analogies to Williams's difficult relationship to "mainstream" poetry institutions, levels a harsher critique of current repressive institutional practices than the complaints I have already made about the reading habits of Altieri and Breslin. In "The Academy in Peril: William Carlos Williams Meets the MLA," Bernstein zeroes in on what he labels "official verse culture":

> Let me be specific as to what I mean by "official verse culture" — I am referring to the poetry publishing and reviewing practices of *The New York Times, The Nation, American Poetry Review, New York Review of Books, The New Yorker, Poetry* (Chicago), *Antaeus, Parnassus,* Atheneum Press, all the major trade publishers, the poetry series of almost all of the major university presses (the University of California Press being a significant exception at present). Add to this the ideologically-motivated selection of the vast majority of poets teaching in university writing and literature programs and of poets taught in such programs as well as the

interlocking accreditation of these selections through prizes and awards judged by these same individuals. Finally, there are the self-appointed keepers of the gate who actively put forward biased, narrowly-focused and frequently shrill and contentious accounts of American poetry, while claiming, like all disinformation propaganda, to be giving historical or nonpartisan views. (247–48)

While Bernstein himself, as a recipient of a Guggenheim grant and an NEA grant, and by virtue of editing a large sampling of poetry in the *Paris Review*, can no longer be considered a complete "outsider," his critique of the institutional practices of the poetry business remains valid:

Official verse culture is not mainstream, nor is it monolithic, nor uniformly bad or good. Rather, like all literary culture, it is constituted by particular values that are as heterodox, within the broad context of multicultural American writing, as any other type of writing. What makes official verse culture official is that it denies the ideological nature of its practice while maintaining hegemony in terms of major media exposure and academic legitimation and funding. At any moment its resiliency is related to its ability to strategically incorporate tokens from competing poetry traditions and juggle them against one another while leaving for itself the main turf. (248–49)

Bernstein's essays (and poetry) point us toward a particular question: "What are the possibilities for a whole that is not constructed along narrative or overtly thematic/historical lines?" (361). But we misunderstand that question if we cordon it off, treating it as merely an aesthetic, formal, stylistic preoccupation. Bernstein hopes that "we can reinterpret Pound's remark that poets are the antennae of the race to mean ideas embodied as poetry construct a new polis in the site of the old: no longer postponed, *enacted*" (379). Bernstein's analysis of the key role played by form (and the renewal of form) in the political practice of writing alerts us to a major problem or contradiction in much of the poetry in our own time that is labeled "political." The problem is *not* that such writing lacks the "intensity" or "craft" or "surprise" of the most accomplished sincere/scenic mode writing, but that politically radical sentiments are often rendered in a received and possibly outmoded (or conservative) style of writing, and presented within an authoritarian model of reading. The problem is with a socially or culturally revolutionary message presented in an authorized, safe form. The style of the writing—inseparable from the text's imagined relationship to a reader—*is* the political action taken in writing; to grant absolute priority to the writing's "message" is to overlook the site where political activity occurs:

> Current literary practice, far from being negated by the recognition of its ideological construction, is liberated by such formulations and can provide models of ideological critique more radical than otherwise available. Literature—art—is the workshop for such models, the research and development sector of culture. It is no accident that cultural work done under the banner of literature has provided the basis for many of the insights of leftist thought. Historically, poetry—as often as not institutionally broken off from the dominant discursive practices of the political thought of the time—has provided a necessary corrective to the crudely rationalistic drifts of much social radicalism and its theory.
>
> There has never been a more urgent need for literature, for in this culture it is primarily in the realm of literature that alternatives to the stale formulas of ideational mimesis and positional writing strategies are being realized. (379)

I can't help concluding that Bernstein's kind of writing involves what Altieri has asked for: poems as "participants in a social drama" (6). And Bernstein's ideas, particularly about the relationship between form and politics or aesthetics and ethics, are bound to be the source of what Breslin claims we don't have today: "ideological disputes" (250). The thoughts on language and representation in *Content's Dream*, as we have seen, are self-consciously and unobtrusively part of a (skeptical) neo-Marxism.

Bernstein's hope and vision for the future centers on the return of language—and the making of meaning—to its users:

> For every mold that is broken, a new one springs up in the midst like Athena out of Zeus's brow. This is a time of great transformation, development, and achievement in the practice of writing in North America. Yet, in North American society as a whole active participation in the shaping of language by its users diminishes every day. That's a very disturbing, but not inevitable, process that must be fought against. (426)

One danger of a standardized language—"correct" writing and its model of lucidity equated with "correct" thought—is that "language is thus removed from the participatory control of its users and delivered into the hands of the state" (26). Which is *not* to say that knowledge of "correct" writing is socially and economically unimportant. When "correct" writing (or a dominant model of poetic expression) begins to be seen, consciously or unconsciously, as the "only" way to write, "the understanding begins to be lost that we are each involved in the constitution of language—that our actions reconstitute—change—reality. . . stripping us of our source of power in our humanness by denying the validity of our power over the constitution of our world through language" (26–27). Thus, for Bernstein, renewed and radicalized attention to matters of language, meaning, and form is not an esoteric activity precisely because

> language is commonness in being, through which we see & make sense of & value. Its exploration is the exploration of the human common ground. The move from purely descriptive, outward directive, writing toward writing centered on its wordness, its physicality, its haecceity (thisness) is, in its impulse, an investigation of human self-sameness, of the place of our connection: in the world, in the word, in ourselves. (32)

But for this connection to take place, I am convinced that the range of our reading must be challenged. And even if our institutional reading habits were to change and include the kind of work put forward by Bernstein, I do not think that our current workshop system could accommodate such a poetics, so fundamental is Bernstein's challenge. With its emphasis on a perpetually overturned style, his is not a poetics susceptible to replication, the key feature of the workshop as analyzed by Hall and Altieri. The invigorating challenge represented by Bernstein's writing leads me to conclude that ours may be a minor age of poetry only in direct proportion to the scope of our reading/consuming (*and* producing) habits; our town may be quiet only in our particular, institutional suburbs.[4]

The crisis in contemporary American poetry stems from the fact that the poetic revolution of the late fifties and early sixties has ceased to invigorate the writing of poetry precisely at the moment when that poetic paradigm finds itself most thoroughly in control of official verse culture. This crisis is compounded by the fact that many poets and critics, while aware of the predominantly dull product being turned out today, are either unaware of or choose to ignore the existence of a counterpoetics of real vitality. While American poetry may be alive and well, its institutionalized form is both terminally ill and well entrenched, circumstances that make for a particularly painful and disputatious moment in our poetry.

Stephen Fredman, in *Poet's Prose: The Crisis in American Verse* (1983), argues that American poetry is always in a state of crisis:

The root meaning of "crisis"—discrimination or decision, a necessary decision—describes the situation of American poetry, which, in a strict sense, has always been in crisis, always called upon to make necessary existential decisions: Will there be an American poetry? How will it differ from or develop from European poetry? What is the place of self and of society in this poetry? American poets characteristically feel themselves called upon to make these decisions, to affirm anew the very vocation of poetry—an act unthinkable (because unnecessary) in Europe. (4)

I have a more specific sense of crisis in mind than Fredman, who does an excellent job of tracing "the paradoxical act of writing poetry in prose" (2). I believe the current crisis is both broader in scope and more narrowly institutional. At the end of his book, in a chapter titled "The Crisis at Present: Talk Poems and the New Poet's Prose," Fredman presents a description of today's poetic climate that I find more accurate than Breslin's view of "our town":

The poetic climate today seems to include as much criticism and philosophy as it does poetry. At present, one finds that ideas, those prime "don'ts" for imagists, radiate excitement and allure. American poets read with poetic appreciation and sometimes envy the prose of Roland Barthes and Jacques Derrida because it is so deeply aware of its engagement with language and with the process of composition yet simultaneously offers ideas and images of great force and currency. . . . Poets today who are writing a new poetry often do so alongside the writing or reading of criticism and are beginning to create a nongeneric poet's prose (or other types of nonlineated poetry) that continues but moves beyond the concerns we have explored thus far. Investigations by contemporary poets no longer concern the boundary between prose and poetry but rather the boundary between literature and factual or theoretical discourse—philosophy, criticism, linguistics, and so forth. (134)

Fredman thus describes the text milieu, if not the ideology, for writers such as Bernstein, Silliman, Antin, and others, a milieu quite removed from the institutionalized poetics of plainspoken emotional sincerity, the self, and the image.

To refocus and draw to a conclusion my own investigation of a crisis in American poetry, I present one final contrasting assessment of our current situation, Mary Kinzie's essay "The Rhapsodic Fallacy" (1984) and Clayton Eshleman's reply (1985). Kinzie's version of today's "bad times" aligns itself with Altieri:

> Contemporary poetry suffers from dryness, prosaism, and imaginative commonplace, but these are hardly its worst features. Rather, the stylistic dullness is disagreeably coarsened and made the more decadent by being a brotherly symptom of, and in fact a technical support for, the assumption (which has only strengthened in the past 150 years) that the aim of poetry is apotheosis, and ecstatic and unmediated self-consumption in the moment of perception and feeling. The flat style is thought of as a kind of private charm that protects the writer against falsehood, insuring his sincerity. But it has tended to take for granted the real content of the inner life, affecting the mannerisms of sincerity without the coherent values that sincerity might express. (63)

Kinzie argues that "nothing is left for us now but a kind of low lyrical shrub whose roots are quick-forming, but shallow" (66). Where Fredman finds the cross-pollenization of poetry and prose revitalizing, Kinzie, like Dave Smith, laments the confounding of "the poetic with the prosaic" (63).

Kinzie makes two important points. She correctly identifies what makes possible today's predominating dull poetry: "For it's not as if the myriad composers of poetry in this country had conspired in their own dullness without the considerable tutelage and support of the readers and critics and teachers of poetry" (70). While the bulk of poetry in any age is probably dull, and while a preponderance of mediocre poetry in and of itself hardly constitutes a crisis, Kinzie correctly implies an institutional focus, through "tutelage," for today's disseminated dullness that can only be broken through a more skeptical, dialectical, and broadened perspective. Kinzie observes that "although they may present no significant barriers to genius, neither do the assumptions and techniques that cooperate in the kind of monotonic poetry we have examined do anything, it seems to me, to encourage, or positively enable, great thought or great poetry" (79). Like Altieri, Breslin, et al., if what she seeks is great thought and great poetry, Kinzie, as Eshleman is quick to point out, needs to take seriously what she excludes from her scope of consideration.

Eshleman's response to Kinzie, which parallels my own response to most critics and poets considered in this essay, is that she ignores the many writers over the past fifty years, continuing into the present [who have] realized in their writing values which she herself espouses, yet claims are absent: complex ideas, the real content of inner life, coherence, and freshness of perception. The most disturbing aspect of her essay is therefore a willful exclusion and a presentation of insignificant contemporary poems as representative of the state of the art. She seems to believe that it is more important to shake her finger at Linda Gregerson and Catherine Rutan than to engage, for example, Robert Duncan and Jerome Rothenberg. (153–54)

As for an alternative capable of avoiding, in Kinzie's words, "monotonic poetry," Eshleman asks, "The moral issue might be put this way: when will critics like Kinzie, Harold Bloom and Helen Vendler start writing on poetry that knows more than they do?" (155). Eshleman concludes with a recommended range for young writers which is quite different from today's institutionalized curricula:

Poetry, as a psychological art, is still in its infancy, and young writers who seek to create great poems in the year 2000 would be better off with texts by Bahktin, Ferenczi, and Hillman, camped along the Amazon, as their workshop, rather than sitting around Argus-eyed, sharpening their defenses in creative writing wards. I, for one, though, fear that the next couple of decades are going to be more populated by schoolmarmish Mary Kinzies than by Blaise Cendrars riding the Transiberian Express. The academic level of Apollonian anxiety appears to feel more and more threatened by the Dionysian rifts and pits that continue to appear in the surface of the century. This means that all of us who believe in a tough, impassioned, critical *and* inspired, world-aware poetry that is not meaninglessly avant-garde or conventionally traditional will have to continually speak out for, and seriously defend, a middle ground. (157)

An irony worth noting is that Kinzie points to Romanticism as the source for today's narrow, lyrical self-expressions. But the Romantics, particularly Wordsworth, Shelley, Keats, and Coleridge, were extremely well read in their contemporary Continental philosophy and not the least bit shy about creating a poetry and prose enriched by deeply speculative thinking. I think it is fair to surmise that if Coleridge were alive today, he would be arguing over the texts of writers such as Derrida, Heidegger, Husserl, and Merleau-Ponty; if Shelley were alive, he'd have writers such as Althusser, Foucault, and Marx at his fingertips.

Such speculations return me to Simpson's remarks with which I began. While I hope my essay demonstrates that not all poets have abandoned "abstract thinking," it should also be clear that many of our most visible and audible poets have. In part, then, the crisis in contemporary poetry stems from the retreat of poets from intellectual labor, which could provide them with a more sophisticated practice of linguistic self-consciousness and hence with more complex forms of social and political intervention. The naïveté of the "personal expression" school is congruent with that of the "language is transparent" school: both show either a willed ignorance or rejection of modern poetic and philosophical history. Yet, their poetic precursors wrote out of unabashedly rich and often "abstract" philosophical concerns. Today's university-trained poet often imbibes an anti-intellectualism that evades the complex issues of language and representation.

In our time, a notion of poetic craft, well described by Altieri and others, has been disseminated. But that craft is dead in the water. The dominant, and institutionalized practice of poetry, as almost everyone concedes, has become dull, repetitive, and narrow. That is precisely why alternative poetics, ignored by Kinzie, Breslin, Altieri, and others, are of such importance.

Today's crisis in American poetry, marked by a broad sense of stagnation and growing critical discomfort, consists of the collision between two incompatible notions of verse practice: one characterized by a plainspoken sincerity, a focus on apotheosis, a single organizing self and/or voice, lyrical brevity, carefully crafted vowel and consonant music, a kind of representational realism, and liberal politics; the other characterized by stylistic innovation, increased attention to the operations of language, enactment rather than re-presentation or summary, a poetry infused with the thinking of modernist and contemporary theory, philosophy, and speculative prose, a more intensely collaborative concept of the reader, and neo-Marxist politics. This collision of opposing poetic models calls for argument, expression, broad reading, and writing. While the turf warfare, because of the economic stakes involved, might be intense, that is not what is significant about this particular moment in our literary history. What excites me is the possibility for a renewed and enlarged poetic practice, a poetry once again fully a part of our intellectual, emotional, and political lives.

Finally, to approach this split in contemporary American poetry from a slightly more conceptual and perhaps less polemical path, what is at issue is a definition (and practice) of postmodernism, a subject recently addressed by Jean-François Lyotard in *The Postmodern Condition: A Report on Knowledge* (1984). Lyotard, considering artistic expression from a broader cultural perspective than my own more narrowly focused attention to poetry, explains:

> A postmodern artist or writer is in the position of a philosopher: the text he writes, the work he produces are not in principle governed by preestablished rules, and they cannot be judged according to a determining judgment, by applying familiar categories to the text or to the work. Those rules and categories are what the work of art itself is looking for. (81)

For Lyotard, as for Bernstein, Fredman, and others, postmodernist expression is characterized by its imperative to "make it new," so that the work of art enacts a questioning of principles of ordering and representation. While Lyotard's examples come from the realm of the plastic and visual arts, his version of postmodernism helps to adjudicate the dispute and crisis that I have been exploring:

> What, then, is the postmodern? What place does it or does it not occupy in the vertiginous work of the questions hurled at the rules of image and narration? It is undoubtedly a part of the modern. All that has been received, if only yesterday (*modo, modo*, Petronius used to say), must be suspected. What space does Cézanne challenge? The Impressionists'. What object do Picasso and Braque attack? Cézanne's. What presuppositions does Duchamp break with in 1912? That which says one must make a painting, be it cubist. And Buren questions that other presupposition which he believes had survived untouched by the work of Duchamp: the place of presentation of the work. In an amazing acceleration, the generations precipitate themselves. A work can become modern only if it is first postmodern. Postmodernism thus understood is not modernism at its end but in the nascent state, and this state is constant. (79)

Lyotard's version of postmodernism bears an important kinship to Bernstein's radical skepticism and to Cary Nelson's vision, by way of Williams (by way of Burr), of "a permanent and celebratory revolution" (Nelson 1981, 23). Rather than emphasizing the, at times, painful instability of such a situation, Lyotard suggests that "the emphasis can also be placed on the increase of being and the jubilation which result from the invention of new rules of the game, be it pictorial, artistic, or any other" (80).

As Fredman emphasizes "a necessary decision" at the root of the word crisis, Lyotard sees today's artist as facing two divergent choices:

> Under the common name of painting and literature, an unprecedented split is taking place. Those who refuse to reexamine the rules of art pursue successful careers in mass conformism by communicating, by means of the "correct rules," the endemic desire for reality with objects and situations capable of gratifying it. . . . As for the artists and writers who question the rules of plastic and narrative arts and possibly share their suspicions by circulating their work, they are destined to have little credibility in the eyes of those concerned with "reality" and "identity"; they have no guarantee of an audience. (75)

Many interdependent forces—economics, audience, publication, "official verse culture" (or "cultural policy"), the marketplace, the university— favor what Lyotard calls "careers in mass conformism" and what I have been calling the conformism of an institutionalized, once revolutionary, poetics. Here is Lyotard's description of some of the forces the postmodernist writer or artist may encounter:

> Artistic and literary research is doubly threatened, once by the "cultural policy" and once by the art and book market. What is advised, sometimes through one channel, sometimes through the other, is to offer works which, first, are relative to subjects which exist in the eyes of the public they address, and second, works so made ("well made") that the public will recognize what they are about, will understand what is signified, will be able to give or refuse its approval knowingly, and if possible, even to derive from such work a certain amount of comfort. (76)

In spite of such threats, ours is a time rich in discomfortingly innovative poetry and poetic thinking. Whether our institutions, which claim to be interested in poetry and in intellectual inquiry, and our academically based poets and critics care to listen is another matter. For the poets and critics whose writing lives are just beginning or still developing, a choice will be unavoidable.

No one is ahead of his time, it is only that the particular variety of creating his time is the one that his contemporaries who also are creating their own time refuse to accept.

—Gertrude Stein

2. Opposing Poetry

"Language" Poetries (Messerli 1987) and *In the American Tree* (Silliman 1986) are the two most important anthologies of contemporary American poetry since Donald Allen's *The New American Poetry* in 1960. They clearly demonstrate that after twenty years of intelligent, ambitious, and persistent literary production Language Writing is no passing fad. Its significance could be greater than any other movement in American writing since the major modernists. Operating outside the universities and the official verse culture, Language Writing has developed a character that makes reviewing it problematic. Detailed readings of its devices and compositional modes might well subordinate Language Writing to the very habits of reading and thought it means to resist. Since the centrality of theory (as coequal to and inseparable from the writing of poetry) distinguishes Language Writing, a review might best serve readers by concentrating on history and principles. As an oppositional literary practice, Language Writing questions the tendencies of mainstream poetry, including its evasion of modernism's formal challenges, its resultant devotion to the plainspoken lyric, and its correlative hostility to philosophy and critical theory. Language Writing specifically takes seriously those theories of the sign and those issues of representation that mainstream poetry repudiates (see, for example, the jeremiad against theory by Peter Stitt [1987]). Language Writing also proposes and makes necessary new methods of reading that force us to reconsider the political dimensions of literary activity.

By the mid-1980s, Language Writing had been either ignored or dismissed by the majority of academic poets and critics. As I argued in Chapter 1 the uneasiness and dissatisfaction expressed in the mid-1980s wave of books and articles on the "crisis" in American poetry are largely made possible, perhaps even assured, by narrow reading habits and restrictive literary politics. For evidence one need only compare the contents of these two anthologies with two others: A. Poulin, Jr.'s *Contemporary American Poetry* (4th ed., 1985) and Helen Vendler's *Harvard Book of Contemporary American Poetry* (1985). There is not a single instance of overlap between the Poulin and Vendler anthologies and the Messerli (1987) and Silliman (1986) collections. My point is not to argue for the "moral" superiority of one grouping over the other; indeed, I am bothered, for example, by the extremely limited representation of African-American writers in the Messerli and Silliman books (especially since the work of writers such as Nathaniel Mackey and Lorenzo Thomas might have been included and, more important, since these alternative anthologies foreground a politicization of the very issue of aesthetic choice). Nor do I wish to be perceived as arguing for a contemporary American poetry curriculum that omits the writing of Adrienne Rich, Robert Lowell, John Ashbery, Michael Harper, James Wright, Lucille Clifton, Louis Simpson, John Berryman, Sylvia Plath, Allen Ginsberg, and others. The argument that I do wish to advance is that anyone who claims to know about contemporary American poetry had better also know about Language Writing.

In his introduction to *"Language" Poetries*, Messerli notes that "since 1976, poets associated in one way or another with this group have published over 150 books of poetry and criticism—demonstrating a resourcefulness and energetic rethinking of the nature of poetry both in social and aesthetic terms" (1). Messerli's anthology presents the work of twenty poets, as well as his own excellent introduction, bibliographical information on each poet, and an extremely helpful list of anthologies and magazines (from 1965 to 1987) that have been dedicated to Language Writing. Wisely, Messerli, both in his selections for the anthology and in his introduction, undermines the presumption that there is or might be "a single definition or a unified complex of ideas which applies to 'Language' poetry" (1).

Silliman's introduction begins with Robert Grenier's essay "On Speech" in the first issue of *This* magazine (1971) and points to a series of magazines, talks, readings, chapbooks, and small press books that developed and disseminated Language Writing. He includes thirty-eight poets in his anthology, dividing the two poetry sections into West and East, identifying the San Francisco Bay Area and a more diffuse East (principally

New York City, but spreading out to Ohio, Virginia, Washington, D.C., and Massachusetts) as main locations for Language Writing. Like Messerli, Silliman includes helpful contributor's notes, but the greatest service and difference of the Silliman anthology is its "Second Front": a section of twenty-three essays, discussions, letters, reviews, and notes. This final section of *In the American Tree* introduces the reader to the inseparability of poetry, prose, and theory in Language Writing, as do the many instances of poetry-in-prose and hybrid texts in both anthologies. (By comparison, Vendler's anthology allows for no prose or hybrids, and Poulin's includes only a very few highly traditional prose poems.)

While Messerli and Silliman each evade and participate in the act of provisionally defining Language Writing, both are less reticent about tracing its social and historical formation. Messerli notes that "through readings, discussions, seminars, personal friendships, and magazines (such as *Tottel's*, *Hills*, *L=A=N=G=U=A=G=E*, *A Hundred Posters*, *This*, *Roof*, *The Difficulties*, and *Poetics Journal*), they [Language poets] have built up a true community of thought that must be the desire of any poet not writing a hermetic verse for his or her eyes alone" (8). This creation of an alternative system of publication and distribution outside of official verse culture and outside of any academic structure is, as Jerome McGann (1987) observed in the *London Review of Books*, one of the most significant aspects of Language Writing. To Messerli's list I would add the magazines *Temblor*, *Lucy and Jimmy's House of "K"*, and *Ottotole*, and the small presses Tuumba, Roof, The Figures, Sun and Moon, and Burning Deck as all being important in sustaining and developing Language Writing. (For a more in-depth understanding of the history and premises of Language Writing, the reader may wish to see three collections of essays: Charles Bernstein's *Content's Dream* [1986], Steve McCaffery's *North of Intention* [1986], and Ron Silliman's *The New Sentence* [1987]).

In his introduction to *In the American Tree*, Silliman (1986) acknowledges a wide range of transformations and challenges (in addition to Language Writing) within American poetry: "Of particular importance has been the full articulation of a literature by, and consciously for, women. Parallel occurences on a smaller scale have taken place within the gay community and those of some ethnic minorities. The pluralization of American writing has permanently altered the face of literature, and for the better" (xxi). The contribution of Language Writing to the pluralization (and decentralization) of American poetry is simultaneously of a political and an aesthetic nature, growing out of a critique of referentiality. Messerli's (1987) introduction and anthology emphasize the aesthetic or stylistic dimension of this critique, as he explains the materiality of Language Writing:

> The poets in this anthology have all foregrounded language itself as the project of their writing. For these poets, language is not something that *explains* or *translates* experience, but is the source of that experience. Language is perception, thought itself; and in that context the poems of these writers do not function as "frames" of experience or brief narrative summaries of ideas and emotions as they do for many current poets. (2)

Messerli's emphasis on the process of signification, what Marjorie Perloff calls the rights of the signifier, points out a substantial split in poetic assumptions with mainstream American poetry, where the heart of the workshop craft is the poet's search for her/his voice. Instead, Messerli writes that "the identity of 'Language' writing itself is less of a fixed point than an 'exploded self' " (8). He cites Craig Watson's conclusion that "such writing serves as 'a performance in which the reader is both audience and performer' " (3) and Bruce Andrews's claim that " 'Language work resembles a creation of a community and of a worldview by a once divided-but-now-fused Reader and Writer' " (4).

The critique of referentiality and the styles of Language Writing are political in nature precisely because of this hope for a radically restructured relationship of writer and reader. By a series of breaks—and it should be noted that none of these establishes a complete break with referentiality—with a unified voice, with a normative grammatical/semantic ordering, with writing organized around theme, with closure, Language Writing resists habitual reading and in that resistance invites the reader to become a producer of the text rather than remain its consumer. (As Silliman, McCaffery, Watten, and others in their essays analyze the issues of authority and economy implicit in such writing, the neo-Marxist element of Language Writing's project becomes explicit.)

Several typical passages from poems included in the Messerli and Silliman anthologies will suggest the challenges posed by Language Writing. The first (which is included in both anthologies) is the beginning of the twenty-eighth section of Lyn Hejinian's *Writing Is an Aid to Memory*:

we are parting with description
termed blue may be perfectly blue
goats do have damp noses

        that test and now I dine drinking with
            others
    adult blue butterfly for a swim with cheerful birds
            I suppose we hear a muddle of rhythms in water
        bond vegetables binder thereof for thread
    and no crisp fogs
                    spice quilt mix
            know shipping pivot
                sprinkle with a little melody
            nor blot past this dot mix
            now for a bit and fog of bath rain
        do dot goats
                swift whipper of rice
    a type as cream
            into a froth
                ranking a time when rain looms

Though the opening line of Hejinian's poem sounds like a typical poem
in the single-voice mode, each succeeding line makes such a method
of hearing the poem inapplicable. Instead of a single speaker and voice
making a "sincere" pronouncement, Hejinian's poem—in the manner of
collage—juxtaposes phrases in a method that entices a reader to consider
the possible relationships between lines. Habitual continuities—of voice
and narrative—no longer guide the poem's movement, and habits of reading (such as the theme-based reading inherited from New Criticism) that
presume unification and closure are resisted by the poet's different exploration of meaning-making. It is not that the poem abandons meaning;
for the "muddle of rhythms," "thread," "fog," "mix," "melody," "mix,"
and "froth" all do suggest that aggregates do occur even in a highly fragmented and seemingly discontinuous semantic realm. Instead, the poem
provokes in the reader a self-consciousness about how we do go about constructing (or taking for granted) continuities in the poem. And while the
poem no longer offers us a single topic that it is "about," the poem does
involve us in a dialectical tension between possible continuities and radical discontinuities. This tension is enacted at both the level of the phrase
and the line: Does the line "goats do have damp noses" continue with
"that test"? are "spice quilt mix" a series of related appositives or unrelated
words placed side by side? Rather than being *about*—"we are parting with
description"—the tension between gathering together and staying apart,

Hejinian's poem embodies those tensions, placing us at the intersection of these two poles of ordering. On the one hand, the tendency to blend exists in "swift whipper of rice / a type as cream / into a froth," and the opposing tendency exists in disjunctive phrases such as "do dot goats" and the injunction "nor blot past this dot mix," which suggests that the individual dots or fragments should not necessarily be assembled within a mosaic which blurs their distinctness.

The second example is the beginning of Charles Bernstein's "Sentences My Father Used":

> Casts across otherwise unavailable fields.
> Makes plain. Ruffled. Is trying to
> alleviate his false: invalidate. Yet all is
> "to live out," by shut belief, the
> various, simply succeeds which. Roofs that
> retain irksomeness. Points at
> slopes. Buzz over misuse of reflection
> (tendon). Gets sweeps, entails complete
> sympathy, mists. I realize slowly,
> which blurting reminds, or how you, intricate
> in its. This body, like a vapor, to
> circumnavigate. Surprising details that
> hide more than announce, shells codifiers to
> anyway granules, leopards, folding chairs.

Though the sound of Bernstein's poem is quite different from Hejinian's—Bernstein's writing has a harsher, more clotted music to it and offers a far less lyrical sound—his poem too immediately departs from the presumption of a single "natural" speaking voice. The title of Bernstein's poem is completely compatible with poems of the scenic mode. But what we get are not typical sentences nor are they the pithy pronouncements that any father would make, unless we begin to understand "the father" as a principle of order-making and exclusion. Rather than as a character, the "father" of Bernstein's poem might best be understood as a limiting force within poetic expression. This contested father might be one who casts an imposing shadow across "otherwise unavailable fields," who demands that a poem "makes plain," and who leads to comfortable and comforting moments in which a speaker in a poem says, "I realize slowly." But Bernstein's poem actively resists any totalizing reading, especially readings based on a single theme constructed upon the scaffolding of a single speaker. It is not that such a poem *fails* to cohere, it resists those (paternal?) codes that enforce simple coherence in favor of exploration of other modes of thinking.

The third example is Tina Darragh's poem "ludicrous stick." Darragh's

ludicrous stick

to
clean
over: T
formal.
whip. b.
or surpass
completion or
etc.: They need
into shape. 6. 1
19) 7. lick the d
stroke of the tongue
by taken up by one str
cream cone. 10. See salt
b. a brief, brisk burst of ac
pace or clip; speed. 12. Jazz.
in swing music. 13. lick and a
perfunctory manner of doing some
time to clean thoroughly, but gave
promise. (ME lick(e), OE liccian; c.
akin toGoth (bi) laigon, L lingere, GK
(up) - licker, n.

Lick (lik), n. a ring formation in the
the face of the moon: about 21 miles in

lick er-in (lik er in), n. a roller on
chine, esp. the roller that opens the st

the card and transfers the fibers to the
Also called taker-in. (n. use of v. phra

licking (lik ing), n. 1. Informal. a.a p
thrashing. b. a reversal or disappointm
2. the act of one who or that which lic

licorice (lik e   ish, lik rish

viewing
point

poem too is not about some prior event that the poem seeks to represent. As the words and the perspective at the bottom of the poem indicate, this poem engages us in the process of establishing a "viewing point." Her poem is partially complicit in dictionary-based methods of precise ordering and defining, but the title and form of Darragh's poem transform such a lens on language into a much more playful—ludicrous, hence ludic— realm. The written nature of "ludicrous stick" collides with the dictionary's information about "lick" as a specific deed of the tongue. And the particular formalism of dictionary language is displayed in Darragh's poem as bumping up against the exuberance and spontaneity of a jazz lick. The shape of Darragh's poem serve to remind us of the partialness—the wedge-like quality—of any perspective we take on language, no matter how thorough or authoritative that approach may claim to be.

The fourth example is the concluding stanza of Bob Perelman's "Seduced by Analogy":

> A nation's god is only as good as its erect arsenal.
> It's so without voice, in front of the face, all my life I,
> In corners, dust, accumulating rage breaking
> Objects of discourse. "Why use words?" Smells from
> The surrounding matter, the whole tamale.
> "I have no idea" "I use my whole body"
> "Be vulnerable" First sentence: They were watching
> The planes to fly over their insurgent hills.
> Second sentence: Their standard of living
> We say to rise. No third sentence.

In the stanza from Perelman's poem, we are most overtly placed in a dimension of poetic language that we can label as "political." But Perelman's writing does not thematize a political perspective nor does the poem offer a political "scene" or anecdote for analysis and emotional catharsis. Rather, the politics under scrutiny—an investigation to be shared by writer and reader—is the politics of modes of discourse and pronouncement. The fuzzy sensitivities of a male learning new modes of "openness"—who may be proud to say "be vulnerable" and to admit "I have no idea"—is an utterly different subject position than that of a country to whom we have applied loaded words like "insurgent" (which inevitably leads to our planes flying over) and for whom we have decided that "their standard of living / We say to rise." Perelman's poem is not about a particular deed in a particular country, but about the rhyming of a mode of subject-object discourse with other deeds of force.

By interrupting our expectations for syntactical completion, each of these passages (in different ways) defamiliarizes the terrain of the poem. No longer the pronouncement of a readily identifiable speaker in an established dramatic moment or scene operating in a voice close to speech and organized within the conventions of the sentence, these representative samples of Language poetry direct our attention to smaller units of signification than theme or sentence: the syllable, the word, and the phrase. For example, the dictionary-derived compositions of Tina Darragh literalize Emerson's pronouncements in "The Poet" that "language is fossil poetry" and "every word was once a poem." Her "ludicrous stick," by virtue of its spatial arrangement, makes the page itself (rather than the line, stanza, or paragraph) a unit for composition. In Hannah Weiner's writing, especially in *CLAIRVOYANT JOURNAL* and *Spoke*, typographical design—italics, changing typefaces, capitalization—register disturbances and discontinuities of thought and composition. Her overwriting or interrupted writing is but one example of the interaction of poets and printers important to Language Writing. Hejinian, the former editor and printer of Tuumba Press, in *Writing Is an Aid to Memory* (1978) creates endless associational possibilities between word, phrase, and line, moving back and forth between the discrete word as "dot" and the "froth" (or "fog" or "mix") of larger verbal patterns of organization. Far from being an arbitrary scattering of words on the page, placement of each of Hejinian's lines is strictly determined by the first letter of the first word. In the examples from Bernstein and Perelman—the former a more radical disturbance of syntax, the latter a mixture of black humor and overt political content—habitual reading is disturbed so that instead of receiving a message or meaning (from writer/producer to reader/consumer), we participate in the construction of meaning, while at the same time the fragmentation invites us to join in resistance to the coerciveness of the cliché, the trendy observation, and the declarative sentence.

Language Writing promises to provoke and sustain a more enriched text milieu for the reading and writing of poetry. This body of writing—by virtue of its attention to an oppositional school within modernism (Williams, Stein, Zukofsky instead of Eliot, Pound, Stevens) and its addition of an original twist to that reading by recourse to European poststructuralism and neo-Marxist criticism—forces us to rethink our relationship to and appropriation of modernist poetry. It also asks us to develop new methods of reading and criticism to come to terms with a poetry emphasizing the signifier. Even so, it might be fair to respond that these theoretical pronouncements sound interesting, but is the poetry any good? My answer is an emphatic yes. While I prefer reading complete texts—such as Silliman's *Ketjak* (1978) and *Tjanting* (1981), Hejinian's *My Life* (1987), Bernstein's *The Sophist* (1987) and *Controlling Interests* (1980), Weiner's *Spoke* (1984), and Perelman's *The First World* (1986)—the poems in both anthologies serve as a fine introduction to the exciting range and production of Language Writing.

Silliman (1987) argues that "what can be communicated through any literary production depends on which codes are shared with its audience" (25). While for many readers, the codes of Language Writing may, at first, seem alien and disconcerting, there is value in overcoming aesthetic xenophobia. Gertrude Stein (1962), who knew well the intensely negative reactions to the new, claims in "Composition as Explanation" that "only when it is still a thing irritating annoying stimulating then all quality of beauty is denied it. . . . If every one were not so indolent they would realise that beauty is beauty even when it is irritating and stimulating not only when it is accepted and classic" (515). Certainly for readers of critical theory Language Writing offers a perhaps overlooked counterpart to those investigations. For readers of mainstream poetry, the stimulus of engagement with an oppositional writing practice—through outraged and expanded reading/writing habits—offers the painful excitement of confrontation and challenge. I hope that these two groundbreaking anthologies will be read with curiosity and enthusiasm, for these collections present to us an important rethinking of the nature of poetry. To ignore this diverse body of writing would be to impoverish our own sense of what poetry is and what poetry can be, as well as our understanding of the present.

3. Poetry Readings and the
Contemporary Canon

The poetry reading, as presently constituted, and especially on American university campuses, plays a small but significant role in legitimizing, judging, and promoting certain varieties of poetry. I do not want to overstate the function or influence of readings in the shaping of a public canon for American poetry. Indeed, sponsored readings are usually granted to poets after they have achieved a certain public stature, and thus the public reading solidifies and/or enhances that stature. Even so, I would like, today,[1] to rethink the functions of the poetry reading with the hope of disturbing and revitalizing that public activity.

Poetry readings, as sponsored by the university,[2] and often with the assistance of the NEA or state branches of the NEA, provide a small income for poets. More important, given the limited resources of most English departments, and thus the limited number of readings presented each year, poetry readings act both as a filtering device—only a few poets can read each year—and as a means of introducing and/or legitimizing the work of a few poets. The legitimizing function gets accomplished in the first few minutes of the reading, as well as in announcements and publicity for the reading: the poet's "professional"[3] credentials are recited and praise for the poet's writing is repeated. The body of the reading—typically, a series of relatively short poems preceded by autobiographical remarks that establish the personal context for the poems' composition—in a less obvious manner legitimizes a particular poetics as well: a plainspoken poetics of a unified "voice." But it is the introduction that most clearly reveals the interlocking network of legitimation: prizes, publications, teaching positions, and fellowships. Charles Bernstein, in a talk delivered at the 1983 MLA convention (repr. in Bernstein 1986), gave this network the label "official verse culture," which he characterized as

> the poetry publishing and reviewing practices of *The New York Times*, *The Nation*, *American Poetry Review*, *The New York Review of Books*, *The New Yorker*, *Poetry* (Chicago), *Antaeus*, *Parnassus*, Atheneum Press, all the major trade publishers, the poetry series of almost all of the major university presses (the University of California Press being a significant exception at present). Add to this the ideologically motivated selection of the vast majority of poets teaching in university writing and literature programs and of poets taught in such programs as well as the interlocking accreditation of these selections through prizes and awards judged by these same individuals. (247–48)

Admittedly, within this more vast and complicated institutional network, the role of poetry readings is fractional.

At one time, perhaps from 1956 to 1976, poetry readings on college campuses did have a revolutionary (or at least disruptive) force to them. They were part of a process of inquiry and exploration, for they were tied to a rejection of certain tenets of high modernist poetry. Poetry readings demonstrated that poetry need not be highly allusive, ironic, impersonal, nor inaccessible. A new poetry, best documented in James Breslin's *From Modern to Contemporary: American Poetry, 1945–1965* (1984), was beginning to take shape and to gain institutional dominance. Poems did not require master explainers; poems could be, again, part of an immediate human community. And it is still possible to idealize and affirm the immediacy of the poetry reading. To do so, I cite remarks (admittedly out of context, for he is advancing a different argument) from Jerome Rothenberg's "The Poetics of Performance":

> My performance is this sounding of a poem: It is renewal of the poem, the poem's enlivening. Without this sounding there wouldn't be a poem as I've come to do it (though, since I work by writing, there would be notes about the poem as I intended it). This is the return to voice, to song, as the poet Gary Snyder speaks of it; it is one side, the impulse toward the oral, toward a poetry of performance, as is that other side, discourse, that the poet David Antin speaks of. Poetry becomes

the sounding—not the script apart, the preparation or notation, but the sounding. Where there's no writing, the sounding truly renews the poem creates it in each instance, for here there's no poem without performance. . . . The poet's delivery may vary, he may read easily or he may falter, he may digress, he may drift at times into a drunken incoherence, he may fulfill or disappoint our expectations of how a poem is spoken. Somehow it's enough that he risked himself to do as much as he could do: to stand there as a witness to his words, he who alone can sound them. . . . The measure of a poem (& much of its meaning) is likewise only clear when it's being sounded: in this case sounded by its maker. The poet when he sounds his poem is witness to the way it goes, the way it came to happen in the first place. (in Vincent and Zweig 1981, 121–22, 123)

Rothenberg writes enthusiastically if overgenerously about what the poetry reading can be, but he is not describing it in its present state. While Rothenberg's remarks can be misapplied as a support for today's mainstream reading, he actually has in mind a more radicalized performance, something more extreme and atypical: an oral ethnopoetics (as in his own presentations), or talk-poems—mixing discourse, questions, and anecdote—as in David Antin's work. The current state of the poetry reading (as an institution and a format) is much closer to Denise Levertov's observations in 1965 in "An Approach to Public Poetry Listenings" (in Levertov 1981). Levertov celebrates the renewed popularity of poetry readings and urges better listening skills for the audiences of such readings. But Levertov (1981) also criticizes an anecdotal and overexplanatory approach by poets reading:

Unconfident of the poem as an existence, created and having its own life and power, they talk about it beforehand as if to conjure it into being. They tell you what it is about, out of what circumstances it arose, what it "tries to say." By the time the poor poem itself gets read, it seems merely a metrical paraphrase of anecdotes already related. (47)

In part because of this anecdotal and personalized format, the dominant version of the poetry reading has become an ossified prop for a certain kind of brief lyric. And, as I shall argue throughout this talk, the range of poets allowed at the academically sponsored podium is alarmingly narrow.

To assess some of the ways in which poetry readings participate in the formation of a public canon for contemporary poetry, particularly the

ways in which university readings act as a filtering device (i.e., which reputations and books will be promoted, and which poetries will be made
audible to university audiences), I have gathered data about a number of
poetry readings. I asked for information from sixty universities:[4] the names
of poets who gave readings on campus during the 1985–86 and 1986–87
academic years, and the sources of funding for these readings (NEA, state,
university, departmental, and so forth). I received replies from twenty-
eight schools: Alabama; University of California at Berkeley; Brown; State
University of New York, College at Buffalo; Columbia; Cornell; Dart-
mouth; Florida; California State University, Fresno; Hawaii; Houston;
Indiana; Louisiana State; Mississippi; Montana; Oberlin; Pennsylvania;
Princeton; San Francisco State; Stanford; Syracuse; Temple; University
of California, Los Angeles; Utah; Virginia; Warren Wilson; Wisconsin-
Madison; and Wisconsin-Milwaukee. Thus, for this two-year period,
1985–87, I have been able to consider the range of poetry included in 400
university-sponsored readings.

After interpreting this data, I contend that the poetry reading, as practiced on the vast majority of university campuses, has become an increasingly narrow public event that offers economic support, as well as the
prestige, publicity, and legitimation of university-sponsored readings, to
that narrowly selected group of poets most willing to affirm the implied
aesthetics of the current poetry reading format. While many different poets
appear on the list that I have gathered—there are 292 different readers—
the aesthetic range is not so vast. Thus, the poetry reading becomes part
and parcel of mainstream poetry's tactics of unacknowledged repression
and exclusion, as well as the mainstream's poorly thought out ideas of form
generally.

As one index for defining rather than merely asserting this aesthetic
narrowness,[5] I have analyzed the responses to my survey by examining
the number of readings given by the poets in two different anthologies:
The Morrow Anthology of Younger American Poets (Smith and Bottoms
1985) and *In the American Tree* (Silliman 1986). I have picked these two
anthologies as an index of comparison for several reasons. Since there is
not a single case of overlapping selection in the two books it is fair to
say these collections represent two different, competing notions of poetry:
the *Morrow* anthology is composed primarily of poets who are teaching
or who have taught in academic creative writing programs; the *Tree* anthology represents a range of East and West Coast experimental poetry

produced outside of the creative writing establishment. Each anthology represents established but midcareer poets,[6] most of whom were born in the period between 1940 and 1950. Of the university-sponsored readings included in my survey, the *Morrow* poets account for seventy-five readings, the *Tree* poets for ten. But the *Morrow* anthology includes many more poets than *Tree*; of *Morrow*'s 104 poets, 40 gave readings; of *Tree*'s 40 poets, 9 gave readings. But such an initial reading of the data is misleading and overgenerous, distorted due to the huge reading series at San Francisco State and its proximity to the varieties of experimentation represented in *Tree*. In fact, eight or nine *Tree* poets who read on campus read at San Francisco State's Poetry Center; eight to ten *Tree* readings took place at San Francisco State's Poetry Center. To put it another way, those *Tree* poets who did get to read at American campuses did not have the chance to reach a new audience, nor was their work legitimated by the American academic network in any broad sense. One conclusion, supported by this data, is that American university poetry reading series for the most part reinforce existing poetic assumptions in a manner that can best be described as xenophobic and exclusionary. I suspect that such a narrow pattern of institutional support reflects the fact that, as Charles Bernstein's analysis of "official verse culture" suggested, poets in and from MFA programs usually choose the poets who are invited to read. The situation is no better if we look at the actions of the primary funding agency for academic reading series, the NEA. Applications for grants to support readings and residencies for the year 1988–89[7] feature the same poets again and again. The result is a relatively stagnant system of funding and patronage, especially disturbing since one of the stated functions of these NEA grants is to introduce new and emerging poets to a broader audience. An NEA panelist told me that the same few poets year after year receive an inordinate share of the NEA's funding. For the 1988–89 grant applications, the names most often repeated (either as proposed and/or previous readers) were Philip Levine, Derek Walcott, Linda Pastan, Gary Snyder, Galway Kinnell, Seamus Heaney, Marvin Bell, Carolyn Forche, Dave Smith, David St. John, Jorie Graham, Tess Gallagher, Sharon Olds, Robert Hass, and Sydney Lea.[8] It is *not* my argument that these are poor poets not worth hearing. But they are not the only ones worth hearing, funding, legitimizing, and, to the limited extent that readings are part of the creation of a public canon, canonizing. I would point out that, while admittedly there are differences in style among the poets whose names appear most frequently on the NEA list and in my own survey results, those poets most frequently proposed for grants and subsequently sponsored to read on university campuses are overwhelmingly the practitioners of a conventional voice-lyric.

The information from the 1988–89 NEA grant applications adds to my argument about aesthetic xenophobia. To follow up on my own focus on the *Tree* anthology as one test of the representation of experimental poetries, of all the NEA-funded series for 1988–89, only one included any representation of *Tree* poets: New Langton Arts, again a reading series based in San Francisco. (Although the New Langton Arts series included a healthy range of experimental writers, it included only one *Tree* poet.) Based on the data I have gathered, I must agree with Charles Bernstein's (1987) claims that

> official verse culture
> of the last 25 years has engaged in militant
> (that is to say ungenerously uniformitarian)
> campaigns to "resist the subversive,
> independent-of-things nature of language"
> in the name of the common voice, clarity, sincerity,
> or directness of the poem
> (33; in Bernstein 1992, 46)

The format for most poetry readings—a brief introduction (usually a mixture of vita and praise), a 45- to 60-minute reading where brief poems are the going thing, with explanations of personal references, some literary references, some circumstances of composition and/or intention—reinforces a narrow conception of poetic accomplishment, further valorizing what Charles Altieri (1984) defines as the "scenic mode" poem (chaps. 1–3), or what Donald Hall (1987) calls the "McPoem." That is, the poetry reading, with a few notable exceptions, exists in complicity with the dominance of the carefully crafted voice-lyric.

What are some alternatives? At a bare minimum, that university support of poetry readings cease to be acts of institutional xenophobia. That is, at a minimum, that a much broader representation be given to the different poetry communities active today: feminist, gay, black, Hispanic, and the broad range of experimental poetries of our time. But why get so concerned with such a call for fairness and range of representation? Because, as Ron Silliman noted in a talk delivered at the New School, New York, 11 November 1988,

The primary institution of American poetry is the university. In addition to its own practices, it provides important mediation and legitimation functions for virtually every other social apparatus that relates publicly to the poem. The university provides the context in which many, and perhaps most, poetry readers are first introduced to the writing of our time; it may even be, as has sometimes been argued, the context in which the majority of all poems in the U.S. are both written and read. (Silliman 1990, 157)

Furthermore, with 2500 colleges and more than 200 writing programs in North America, college course reading lists constitute the largest single market for books of poetry (Silliman 1987). Or, as Robert von Hallberg (1985) suggests, "the audience for poetry can be identified to a considerable extent with one particular set of social institutions: colleges and universities" (22). With the development and increased vitality of small press publishing and distribution, one way to describe the development of American poetry over the past twenty-five years is as a process of increased decentralization. As Silliman (1987) suggests, today we have a situation of "decentralization in which any pretense, whether from the 'center' or elsewhere, of a coherent sense as to the nature of the whole of American poetry is now patently obvious as just so much aggressive fakery" (172). Access to a greater range of audible, public poetries matters because poetries must be understood as "socially competing discourses" and because the academy is and ought to be "a ground, a field for contestation" (Silliman 1990, 154, 165).

As practiced at present, the academic poetry reading circuit is a narrowly constituted prop for the dominant craft of the workshop — the poem that I have been referring to as a voice-lyric. As Bob Perelman (1988) argues,

> The workshops' commitment to "voice" as immediate, authentic subjectivity is similar to the royal we of the [Harold] Bloomian audience in that it masks the institutional circuits, the networks of presses, reviews, jobs, readings, and awards that are the actual sounding board of voice. Its unity is guarded jealously. . . . The voice may be introspective or even tortured with doubt, but its cohesiveness is never in doubt.

Such assumptions about voice are but one aspect of the poetry reading that I would like to see put into question. Charles Bernstein argues for poetry to "be understood as epistemological inquiry" (1987, 12; 1992, 17–18). As David Antin's talk-poems, and their subsequent transcriptions, enact so disquietingly, the public poetry reading presents an ideal occasion to problematize the location and the nature of the poem. Thus, I find it doubly ironic that the dominant reading format idealizes the presentation of voice yet manages to exclude nearly absolute practitioners such as David Antin of a "pure" or more radicalized form of voice- or talk-poetry. While my data analysis emphasizes a comparison of *Morrow* versus *Tree* readings, the problem of aesthetic bias in university-sponsored readings is much broader than a "university poet" versus Language poet dispute. Poets such as Antin (whose talk-poems call into question the poem's and the poetry reading's all too readily assumed conventions), other performance artists, and a wide range of other poetic innovators are also being excluded from the university-sponsored podium. Readings can and should be part of a broader act of poetic exploration and inquiry. But today that opportunity is being forfeited. So long as poetry readings remain a habitualized form of entertainment, the site of institutionally narrow acts of representation, and the ritualization of brief personalized expression, the poetry reading is condemned to a non-self-reflective act of formal repetition. To reinvigorate the format and the content of poetry readings, to renew the heuristic function of the poetry reading, I suggest careful attention to the implications of Jerome Rothenberg's questions and assertions in "The Poetics of Performance":

> What do we say about the function of our poetry, the thing we do? That it explores. That it initiates thought or action. That it proposes its own displacement. That it allows vulnerability & conflict. That it remains, like the best science, constantly open to change: to a continual change in our idea of what a poem is or may be. What language is. What experience is. What reality is. (in Vincent and Zweig 1981, 125)

When poetry readings cease to propose their own displacement, we wind up with the present situation, where the variety of names masks the sameness of conception and the narrow range of institutional support. Instead of a risk-taking venture that enlivens the process of forming a public canon for contemporary poetry, we wind up with a predictable event that no longer disturbs or challenges its participants. We get a version of the poetry reading that reinforces a narrow spectrum of written and verbal expression.[9]

till other voices wake

us or we drown

    —George Oppen

> The anxiety to invent an "American" nation and the anxiety to invent a
> uniquely "American" literature were historically coincident. As long as we
> use "American" as an adjective, we continue to reenforce the illusion that
> there is a transcendental core of values and experiences that are essentially
> "American," and that literary or cultural studies may be properly shaped by
> selecting objects and authors according to how well they express this
> central essence.
>
>   —Gregory Jay

4. The Politics of Form and Poetry's Other Subjects

Reading Contemporary American Poetry

It is not possible to write *the* history of contemporary American poetry,
though it is, of course, worthwhile to attempt to historicize the present.
Nearly twenty years ago in the first issue of *Boundary 2*, David Antin
(1972) claimed that "it is precisely the distinctive feature of the present
that, in spite of any strong sense of its coherence, it is always open on its
forward side" (98–99). In 1990, a writer who attempts both to be in the
present and to formulate the crucial activities in poetry must feel that open
forward side as well as the inevitably partial nature of any individual's attempted formulation. Having admitted the impossibility of the task, and
having acknowledged that a dream of inclusivity would itself have serious
liabilities and hidden partialities, I find few tasks so important as an engaged reading of contemporary American poetry.

    The decentralization of literary production in the United States calls
for an active reception in which readers share discoveries and information.
Today, there is a great deal of good poetry that is not being read. To think
about contemporary American poetry, with any attempt at comprehen-
siveness and seriousness, brings a writer in contact with a range of controversies. The criticism of contemporary poetry is usually given over either to
aesthetically dominated judgmental reviews (mainly short blurbs of praise
written by peer-poets implicated in the literary/professional networks they
are asked to judge) or to an academically sanctioned (mis)application of

current critical theory to canonically (and professionally) acceptable extended readings of "major" contemporary poets.

In spite of this dismal state of institutionalized criticism of poetry, a number of recent books on contemporary American poetry *are* adventurous and valuable. Of nine books under consideration in this chapter, all are provocative, and eight of the nine extend into that open forward side of contemporary American poetry. Considered collectively, recurring topics and points of controversy emerge. I am surprised to find that debates over the meanings and implications of the "postmodern" in contemporary poetry have not (with the exception of some of Andrew Ross's work) been very productive or interesting. What surfaces instead is an intense struggle over the canon of contemporary American poetry, especially in light of an active rethinking of the nature of the self and the importance of what is called (after Lacanian psychoanalysis) subject position. As nearly all of the books I examine demonstrate, two overlapping areas of thinking emerge as pivotal to a consideration of contemporary American poetry. The first is the dissemination of "the subject," accomplished variously by formal innovation, theoretical argument, and multicultural studies. The second is the politics of poetry as a *resistance to appropriation*: resistance to the official verse culture, the marketplace, the dominant culture, and hegemonic ideologies.

A broad awareness of the decentralization of poetry production, as well as an established critique of the limited nature of today's professionalized and institutionalized poetry writing, have had a salutary effect on attempts to describe contemporary American poetry. The most fruitful areas of thought are those that begin from a multicultural perspective and those that theorize the relationship of form and politics, where form is considered broadly as an institutional and social practice as well as an aesthetic set of choices.

The book jacket for J. D. McClatchy's *White Paper: On Contemporary American Poetry* (1989) puts forward the claim that his book is "an incisive survey of contemporary American poetry . . . an overview of the current poetry 'scene' . . . [and] a book designed to help us . . . to discriminate the best from the weaker work in a crowded and difficult field." Apparently McClatchy has found an easy way to do so: eliminate from consideration most of the challenging work of the day. Eliminate writing by poets of "otherness," especially color or innovation. In *White Paper*, McClatchy presents a regional, class, and aesthetic appreciation masquerading as "the tradition" and "the best."

McClatchy (1989) claims, "I bear no ideological grudges. In fact, my brief is against those who would make American poetry over into images of any narrow critical orthodoxy. Ours is a heritage of heresies" (viii). And the ideology of no ideology is one such heresy. I do share, however, one of McClatchy's grudges: opposition to the leveling effect of "the middlebrow expectation brought to poetry over the past thirty years by critics and poets alike" (viii). That particular complaint has been thoroughly developed already by Charles Altieri, Donald Hall, and fifty others (and is discussed in the first chapter of *Opposing Poetries*). But what of McClatchy's concealed ideology? It rests with an unstated preference for the bourgeois subject and with notions of individual psychological development: "If to help understand them [the poets] I have sometimes turned to modern mythographers like Freud and Jung, that is because the poets themselves have shaped their stories into patterns that psychology had most vividly drawn for them" (ix). That is the funnel through which McClatchy sifts contemporary American poetry to come up with his list of the greatest of the day.

Along the way McClatchy dismisses the terms "academic" and "avant-garde" as bankrupt, failing to realize that his own position is that of the academic par excellence (or, more discriminatingly, the high academic, with the workshop/middlebrow being the low or populist academic). He also fails to grant that there is anything besides an academic poetry, and thus he can fail to locate a significant avant-garde. In his scorn for a "permissive era" of poetry writing, he asks, "what *could* shock or muster these days?" (8). I have three quick responses: Language writing, Antin's talk-poems, and the use of black idiom by poets like June Jordan.

Even so, McClatchy proves capable of questions and assertions that thought about from some of the other perspectives I shall introduce in this chapter, can be fruitful. McClatchy argues, "Poetry's work of knowledge and its access to power lie in the poet's instinct, as well as in the reader's capacity, to take *poesis* itself—its repertory of song, choice, play, pattern, logic, trope—and see it as a model of experience, and use it as the means to fathom those same sources of authority and transformation in our lives" (15). The problem with this admirable formula is that the "model of experience" it presumes is highly provincial. It cannot provide an acceptable answer to his inquiry into poetry as knowledge. Again and again, McClatchy returns to a model of the bourgeois subject, in a kind of isolated meditation, mulling over the nature of his individual experience (typically narrated with wit, decorum, and closure). The terrain which McClatchy defends is not that of "great" poetry, but that which conforms to an ideology of the self: "More eloquently than any other advocate, Harold Bloom has argued that poetry is precisely that sanction: the defense of the self against *everything*—ideology, history, nature, time, others, even against the self, and especially against 'cultural force'—that might destroy it. If the best poetry today seems more demanding or eccentric than it did when Longfellow, or even Whitman, was writing, so are the conspiracies against the self" (15–16).

Conspiracies, or best thoughts about what that self is (and is not)? Or best thoughts about how else to write, rather than producing a stable self and a personal voice? That McClatchy's is indeed an ideology of the self, and an elevation of that self over and above competing conceptions, becomes most readily apparent in his reading of Robert Lowell's work: "History is, after all, a series of biographies, a series of readings. Lowell's historical quest gives way, finally, to his struggle with the family romance, and his effort is to reconcile history with the self, and thereby gain control over both" (138).

There are serious problems with what McClatchy authenticates as those poems worthy of his reading talent and, by extension, ours too. He is willing to reduce poetry to a matter of voice (which is really only a subcategory of his ideology of the self): "We speak excitedly of a distinctive 'new voice' only when it can be distinguished from all the others. Whole movements in poetry are matters of voice, whether two hundred years ago when 'poetic diction' was the operative term, or right now when the Language poets or the New Formalists are speaking up for themselves" (25). Wrong. Especially about the Language poets, who have each in *many* different ways put the notion of voice itself into question and have written (again, in divergent ways) poetry that has little to do with "voice" at all.

McClatchy's reading of Elizabeth Bishop's poetry—which satisfies his definition of great poetry as having the quality of "austere grandeur" (68)—reveals the dullness and predictability of his method: "I want now to read through the poem ["The End of March"], and listen for allusions that add to the sense of it. . . . If we can't hear the allusions she is subtly making—and her early readers did not—then we can't estimate the true power of the poems—their thematic ambitions, their autobiographical bearings, the rightful place they should assume in the traditions of American poetry" (56, 57). Theme, the story of the self, and the poet's ranking: these equal the true power of poetry? When filtered through a high modernist and Anglophile reading list of accredited allusions, the result is a dull, smug, arrogant "white paper." A sort of aesthetic and cultural apartheid.

By contrast, what is refreshing about Stephen-Paul Martin's *Open Form and the Feminine Imagination* (1988), and several other books I shall be discussing, is the effort to break discussions of poetry out of a narrowly defined psychological aestheticism (inherited from New Criticism, and absorbed seemingly without a qualm by McClatchy). Martin's way out is via an increased attention to "the extra-literary relevance" (60) of the writers he considers: Gertrude Stein, Hart Crane, Wallace Stevens, Djuna Barnes, Clarence Major, Carla Harryman, Susan Howe, Ron Silliman, and Teresa Cha. Nevertheless, the principal tool of New Criticism—close reading—often remains the dominant methodology for Martin, and indeed for most historicized, cultural, political, and theoretical approaches to contemporary American poetry. So too does thematization come in as a ghostly essentialism that reins in more adventurous varieties of criticism. These difficulties are not so much failings of individual critics as they are indicative of a generic difficulty in writing criticism of contemporary poetry.

Despite its unconventional intentions, Martin's book remains bound up in its own dualisms and essentialisms: female/male, open/closed, intuitive/rational, body/mind. Even while advocating a "female" perspective, Martin does so by traditionally "masculine" methods of assertion and argumentation. Also, he is beholden to an evolutionary and developmental model: "I also think that a technologically advanced and politically aggressive (masculine) country like the United States should be aware that it is capable of evolving past its current patriarchal limitations, and that some of its writers—both men and women—have already done so" (56).

Clearly, there is an important pedagogical dimension to Martin's choice of texts. The works he considers force us into different kinds of reading, thinking, and questioning. As such, avant-garde writing ought generally to occupy an important place in all curricula on heuristic and political grounds. As Martin's book demonstrates, reactions to experimental writing matter as engagements with fundamental habits of inclusion and exclusion, as crucial instances of treatment of the "other," and as tests of our tolerance of a broad range of ways to "make sense."

But Martin's claims for the innovativeness of the texts are not matched by new habits of reading and critical writing. The "enemy"—a kind of narrow-minded version of logical, causal thinking—is repeatedly identified. But, as in the Stevens chapter, even when Martin's thematization is profeminine and antipatriarchal, his own criticism remains insistently thematic and thus not so different from the thinking that he criticizes: "We are so trained to conceptualize according to definitions and classifications, fitting them neatly into cause and effect patterns, that anything else seems incomprehensible" (92). Typical of Martin's essentialism is his classification of Stevens' "fat girl" (in "Notes Toward a Supreme Fiction"): "She is that opulent, warm, and fertile essence associated with the Great Mother and the darkness of nonrational expression" (93).

Martin searches for a radical innocence through the deconstruction of masculine dominance. In discussing Major's work, Martin argues that fragmentation "is a way of de-composing the 'ceremony' of masculine domination so that a more authentic form of innocence can emerge" (121–22). Elsewhere, he argues that "the 'difficulty' of poetry is that it will not serve the assumptions of a society based on material prestige" (95). But such a statement is only partially true; as a more rigorously Marxist or materialist approach (by Hartley, Kalaidjian, or Silliman) would have us consider, poetry too, as a mode of production and a social/political activity, has its own particular material conditions that we should scrutinize.

One great strength of Martin's book (and the magazine he co-edits, *Central Park*) is his ability to link up, intelligently, "post-rational science and post-modern writing" (139). He deserves high praise for fine readings of and introductions to the writing of Harryman, Howe, and Cha. The goal he achieves, which others could strive for, is a multiculturalism *within* a consideration of innovative writing. Too often, multicultural readings are restricted to "natural" language styles only or to the opposite segregation: experimental writing as the province of whites only. Not so in Martin's provocative book.

In a somewhat less polemical version of cultural criticism, but one that chooses a more formally conservative set of texts for consideration, Walter Kalaidjian in *Languages of Liberation: The Social Text in Contemporary American Poetry* (1989) examines the institutional and social setting of recent American poetry by way of Adorno and other cultural critics. Kalaidjian's most important contribution lies in his analysis of the persistent critical methodologies derived from New Criticism:

> Despite the outpouring of rhetoric dubbing postwar verse a "poetry of revolt," its reception was marked by the foundational oppositions of New Critical doctrine: poetry enjoys an aesthetic autonomy from its institutional infrastructures; the "ideal reader" transcends heterogeneous interpretive communities: and the private lyric voice dwells apart from history's social text. . . . [P]oetic autonomy, "disinterested" reading, and

voice dominated the center of the New Critical enterprise by marginalizing history, audience, and textuality. (13)

Kalaidjian, like George Hartley in *Textual Politics and the Language Poets*, concludes that "From our vantage point in the 1980s, this theoretical failure can be mapped as the period's political limit: one that actively led readers to invest in ideologies of bourgeois individualism" (14).

Kalaidjian demystifies the role of "poet" by considering this subject position in its institutional and commercial setting. He studies the conglomerate publishing business, mass media, and the networks of prestige and awards tied into the most commercially visible means of publication. He also considers the specific career options and publishing choices made by poets such as Robert Bly, Adrienne Rich, and Gwendolyn Brooks. Such information, as well as Kalaidjian's comments, helps desanctify the reading of contemporary poetry and makes material and commercial matters an essential part of reading a poet's work.

In accordance with Silliman's observations, Kalaidjian too observes that "The nexus between academe and poetry writing is vital to the formation of the postwar verse canon" (20). Kalaidjian, to his credit, willingly assesses the harsh consequences of a poet's institutional setting. He admits and analyzes the hypocritical position of most mainstream, canonically accepted, academic poets: "Today literature's humanizing rhetoric is often belied by its actual disciplinary formations and institutional limits. This tension continues to be most deeply felt by academics, whose everyday professional lives deny the consoling models of community that humanism traditionally espouses. For better or worse, most of our enduring verse writers are academics whose poetry typically seeks to repress and transcend their institutional lives" (26–27).

Kalaidjian offers critical, intelligent readings of the work of James Wright and W. S. Merwin, but even these fine readings fail to develop adequately the material readings that Kalaidjian advocates. Throughout his own book, Kalaidjian too falls victim, in varying degrees, to New Critical blindnesses. He does not, for example, really consider the material and institutional settings for Wright and Merwin, failing to wonder about Wright's resistance to the workshop format, his revulsion at abstract critical thinking, his interest as a scholar in the work of Dickens and the nineteenth-century novel generally; nor does he consider why Merwin changed publishers for *Finding the Islands*, nor Merwin's ambivalent but lucrative relationship to foundations and academic financial support networks. Kalaidjian's own readings often merely substitute contemporary theoretical language for the isolationist aestheticism of New Criticism.

A more serious failing is his often essentialist and uncritical use of the term "cultural critique." In an excellent concluding chapter—excellent both for its insights and for attending to the work of an important but neglected poet—he praises Brooks for employing "her poetry . . . as a discursive medium for cultural critique" (173). But throughout his book "cultural critique" remains a term of praise rather than a category for analytical thinking. Could it not be argued that virtually all poetry participates in cultural criticism? As with Martin's difficulty in overcoming a thematic criticism, I see Kalaidjian's essentializing of the term "cultural criticism" as a generic difficulty for criticism of contemporary American poetry.

More important, Kalaidjian's own forms of institutional blindness seriously jeopardize his project. He maintains a narrow version of accepted texts to reflect social and cultural criticism. If, as he claims, one of his chief interests is to study poets' interrogation of "the bourgeois myth of the sovereign subject" (123), how can Kalaidjian deny attention to the work of a number of Language poets? Bob Perelman, Silliman, Charles Bernstein, Barrett Watten, and a host of other poets have spent nearly twenty years investigating this precise area of concern. Especially given Kalaidjian's attention to the Frankfurt School (crucial to the work of Silliman) and to the work of Charles Olson, this omission (as Silliman and Bernstein have written important essays on Olson) is all the more puzzling. Kalaidjian's reading of Olson would be deepened by consideration, for example, of Bernstein's critique of Olson's masculinist biases.

Kalaidjian thus dodges writing that would extend and challenge his own analysis of the expressive voice-lyric's failings, the commercial and institutional setting of contemporary American poetry, and the critique of the bourgeois subject. So, too, would his consideration of a feminist poetics be enhanced by attention to work more formally adventurous than that of Rich, who he sees as practicing what the French call *l'écriture féminine*: "Like Kristeva, Rich invokes the word's somatic body, the libidinal force of the semiotic normally repressed from the symbolic economy of language" (164). While Kalaidjian justly praises Rich's many changes in style, one must also admit that Rich's work remains based on models of thematic coherence, unity, and relatively straightforward transmission of a message. Why not read such cultural criticism, organized thematically, beside the more formally adventurous and innovative work of poets such as

Susan Howe, Rachel Blau DuPlessis, and Beverly Dahlen? Overall, Kalaid-jian's book, with its basis in cultural criticism, points toward an important (though only partially fulfilled) way of reading contemporary American poetry.

The Politics of Poetic Form: Poetry and Public Policy, a collection of essays edited by Charles Bernstein (1990), extends the critique of the bourgeois subject advocated by Kalaidjian by focusing on the political implications of a poem's formal dynamics. Bernstein declares in the book's preface:

> Poems are imagined primarily to express personal emotions; if political, they are seen as articulating positions already expounded elsewhere. In contrast, poetry can be conceived as an active arena for exploring basic questions about political thought and action. . . .The particular focus of this collection is on the ways that the formal dynamics of a poem shape its ideology; more specifically, how radically innovative poetic styles can have political meanings. (vii)

Instead of McClatchy's white Northeastern, Norton British Lit lineup of poets, we are urged to consider the range implied by Jerome Rothen-berg's term "ethnopoetics," which "refers to an attempt to investigate on a transcultural scale the range of possible poetries that had not only been imaged but put into practice by other human beings" (5), a range confirmed and disseminated by Rothenberg's twenty years of making anthologies. Rothenberg concludes that "the multiple poetries revealed by an *ethno*poetics lead inevitably to the conclusion that *there is no one way*; thus, they contribute to the desire/need already felt, to undermine authority, program, & system, so as not to be done in by them in turn" (9). Rothenberg, from a position outside Kalaidjian's "languages of liberation," describes a language poetics that is "a way of life. An instrument . . . of *liberation*. A private/public healing," stemming from the fact that "I *see* through language" (13).

In contrast to McClatchy's commonsensical notions about the self, we have Bruce Andrews's (1990) formulations in "Poetry as Explanation, Poetry as Praxis," which would "define comprehension as something other than consumption" (28). He argues, "If identification is built into the subject-form—so that its positive meanings are already overproduced— then 'subjects speaking their minds' 'authentically' will not be enough. The overall shape of making sense needs to be reframed, restaged, put back into a context of 'pre-sense'—to reveal its constructed character; to reveal by critique, by demythologizing. Otherwise, its apparent immediacy dupes us: the lack of distance is a kind of closure" (31–32).

The act of *poesis* figures into a social resistance for Bernstein in the particular way that poetry reconvenes a public for the choosing of conventions for "acceptable" communication: "Don't get me wrong: I know it's almost a joke to speak of poetry and national affairs. Yet in *The Social Contract*, Jean-Jacques Rousseau writes that since our conventions are provisional, the public may choose to reconvene in order to withdraw authority from those conventions which no longer serve our purposes, & poetry is one of the few areas where this right of reconvening is exercised" (240–41).

But for questions of canon formation and the institutionalization of poetry, Silliman's "Canons and Institutions: New Hope for the Disappeared" (1990) is one of the most provocative essays written in quite some time. Silliman (1990) asserts that "poetry, particularly in the United States, is an amnesiac discourse" (150). Poets and poetry are read (or not) and discarded at an alarming rate: "The shelf life of a good poet may be something less than the half-life of a styrofoam cup" (150). A chief means of erasure is "the process of public canonization, that which socially converts the broad horizon of writing into the simplified and hierarchic topography of Literature" (152), a disease he refers to elsewhere as "canonic amnesia or Vendler's Syndrome" (169). But Silliman's argument is not a mushy pluralism, "in which all poems would be equal for all readers" (152). Instead, he wishes (as do many of the poets identified as Language poets) to make ideology and form apparent and at issue in poetry, and thus to make the choices and partiality of what we value in poetry more visible and open to argument. For Silliman, "value . . . is a definable relationship":

> What it is not, however, is a conjunction between tradition and the individual talent. For in and of itself, tradition is nothing: it does not exist. Tradition is a bibliography with implications. It is what one has read and how one links these together. And not just any One, but each and every specific person, that potentially infinite regress of subject positions. Thus one cannot define value without specifying the reader at stake: valuable for whom? to what end? (152–53)

Silliman reminds us that a canon (or a syllabus or a book claiming, as McClatchy's does, to survey contemporary American poetry) involves "socially competing discourses" (154). He argues that "the survival of poets and poetry are determined institutionally rather than between texts or aesthetic principles" (157). Syllabus decisions, invitations to poets to read on campus, and decisions about which poetry to review and which poets will be covered in a book or essay are all important choices because, as Silliman notes, the university "provides important mediation and legitimation functions for virtually every other social apparatus that relates publicly to the poem. The university provides the context in which many, and perhaps most, poetry readers are first introduced to the writing of our time; it may even be, as has sometimes been argued, the context in which the majority of all poems in the U. S. are both written and read" (157). As Silliman continues later in his essay, "the academy is a ground, a field for contestation" (165). So we must make sure that it *is* and that other voices are invited into the field for contestation.

Silliman proposes the tactic of "aesthetic practice raised to an institutional strategy" (169). Such action would involve questioning the institutionalized separation of theory and practice, redrawing (or erasing) boundaries between critical and creative writing, "deconstructing public canonicity and rejoining theory to practice" (167), and "a pluralization of the poetry publishing programs of university presses—a level of the academy that is even more arthritic and senile than MFA programs" (169). To this end, Silliman underscores a chief value of Bernstein's anthology; *The Politics of Poetic Form* offers sharply drawn perspectives on poetry's American institutionalization from a series of vantage points outside that institutional framework.

George Hartley's *Textual Politics and the Language Poets* (1989), the first book-length study of Language poetry, does not pretend to be a comprehensive, nonideological survey of what is of value in contemporary American poetry. He examines Language poetry as a critique of bourgeois society. Like many of the contributors to *The Politics of Poetic Form*, Hartley excels in analyzing the relationship of poetic form and politics. Hartley develops his study out of careful readings of Althusser, Benjamin, Brecht, de Saussure, Jameson, Lukács, Kristeva, and Marx. If there is an abiding weakness to his book, it is his tendency to get bogged down in arguments over fine points of Marxist theory. It is a slight oversimplification to say that the poetry gets lost in the shuffle, because such whining from a reviewer usually presupposes a split between poetry and theory, but the complaint, even from one sympathetic to the poetics of poetry *as* poetry, is still one that must be lodged against Hartley's book.

Hartley understands that Language poetry, among other things, represents a rebuke of the "voice-poem," "the dominant model for poetic production and reception today." For many Language poets "the voice poem depends on a model of communication that needs to be challenged: the notion that the poet (a self-present subject) transmits a particular message ('experience,' 'emotion') to a reader (another self-present subject) through a language which is neutral, transparent, 'natural'" (xii). Language poets propose poetry as "the exploration of the possibilities for meaning-production" (xiii). Hartley argues, "Language poets have developed a poetry that functions not as ornamentation or as self-expression, but as a baring of the frames of bourgeois ideology itself" (41).

Hartley's study, which thinks *within* the framework of Language poetry, theorizes the political significance of current rethinking of the subject: "Poetry, then, which functions according to the notion of the poet/speaker as an independent subject who, having 'found his voice,' presents a situation seen from a single point of view, fosters the key ideological concept of bourgeois society: the self-sufficient, self-determined individual free to participate in the marketplace" (37). Hartley's analysis of signification and the subject results in an understanding crucial to any conceptualization of an avant-garde. It is not the newness of a method but the oppositional nature—socially, institutionally, politically—of that art that makes of it a vanguard, for it represents "those who challenge their time's hegemonic conceptualization of art" (1). As such, Hartley's reading of Language poetry is correctly "traditional," exploring various Language poets' rereadings of writers such as Stein, Olson, and Williams.

The crux of Hartley's analysis is the claim that meaning, reference, and signification are socially contracted understandings. They are conventions with ideological implications (owing to the inevitable commodification of language products), arrived at by readers and writers through institutionally mediated methods. Reference, meaning, even "excellence," result not from some quality inherent in the poem. Instead, "reference is thus to be seen as the end result of the social process of language production, not as the inherent quality of the words themselves" (34).

Though Hartley does not stumble into the worn path of theme study and tedious middlebrow close readings, he does get led astray by one of the truisms of critical approaches to Language poetry. Hartley tends to stop with the generalization that with Language poetry the reader becomes a collaborator in the production of meaning. We get only scant evidence of what this might mean in practice. Rather than draw this pat conclusion, which really amounts to an assertion of preference for Language writing (and thus might be one more aesthetic judgment), Hartley and other critics of Language poetry (myself included) would do well to begin with the kinds of questions Hartley himself poses elsewhere in his book: "What is the *meaning* of our particular uses and conceptions of meaning at our particular historical juncture? To whose benefit is the present definition of meaning put?" (70).

Hartley's book overlaps with the work of Perloff and Sayre in its reference to the theories of other modernist artists, a set of references that takes us beyond poetry to the visual and plastic arts. Hartley's discussion of conceptual art implies the kind of question to be asked today about poetry: "The Conceptualists therefore turned to less 'material' matter, such as water, inert gas, or ultimately simply ideas, in a process of increasing 'dematerialization' of art. The original conception, the idea, the intention of the artist *is* the work" (85). Such an observation, and such a context for the consideration of contemporary American poetry, leads us, as Sayre also does, to wonder where in fact the work of art, where the poem, most fundamentally takes place, when is its crucial moment, and where is it found. Such questions lead us back into debates of product versus process, but they also give us new contexts for appreciating a broader range of poetry: from Antin's talk-poems and skywriting poems, to Jenny Holzer's visual displays, to Rothenberg's performance-rituals, to the typographical experimentation of Johanna Drucker and Tina Darragh—all poetry that relies on a more open notion of where and how the poem takes place. As electronic and other digitalized modes of production supplement or replace the book, such rethinking of poesis may well prove crucial to a sustained interest in poetry itself.

Marjorie Perloff's *Poetic License: Essays on Modernist and Postmodernist Lyric* (1990) extends her "ongoing project" of writing "a revisionist history of twentieth-century poetics" (2). Some of the best work in this book consists of readings of specific poets' work: Howe, Niedecker, Ginsberg, McCaffery, Beckett, Plath, and the legacies of Pound. Perloff is sometimes mistakenly labeled merely a theoretician of the avant-garde, when in fact her readings are often empirically based. Her most intriguing empirical chapter in *Poetic License* is "*Traduit de l'Américain:* French Representations of the 'New American Poetry.'" While several critics have pointed out the competing and mutually exclusive versions of contemporary American poetry by comparing anthologies such as *In the American Tree* (Silliman 1986) to Vendler's (1985) Harvard anthology or the Morrow anthology (Smith and Bottoms 1985), Perloff seeks out an external point of reference in these anthology/canon struggles. She presents persuasive evidence for a French version of contemporary American poetry that differs considerably from the predominant American erasure of the Pound-Williams-Stein tradition. As Perloff demonstrates, French readings and translations of contemporary American poetry emphasize the work of Stein, Zukofsky, Rothenberg, Spicer, Cage, Palmer, the Beat poets, and the work of many Language poets. What is at stake in competing versions of contemporary American poetry, as Kalaidjian, Hartley, and others have asserted from an *intra*national viewpoint, is a refutation of the personal voice-poem. Perloff finds the French poets, anthologists, and translators barely interested in our mainstream voice-based poems, having lost interest in poems of "the 'I-as-sensitive-register'" (63) and "late English-Romantic lyrics in which a particular self meditates on the external scene and moralizes the landscape" (61).

A contemporary poetry that interests Perloff begins with the understanding "that Romantic subjectivity is itself a cultural construction whose relevance to modernist poetics is questionable" (80). Perloff demonstrates that the critique of bourgeois subjectivity in poetry is inevitably linked to a rethinking of the possibilities and nature of the lyric. She argues persuasively for the displacement of the lyric, either through radically rewriting it or by discarding it altogether, as a significant development in contemporary (innovative) poetry.

Silliman's argument that American poetry is an amnesiac discourse finds considerable support in Perloff's reading of Merwin's poetry. Merwin's work was and is (see for example Kalaidjian's chapter on Merwin) praised for its adventurous forms. But Perloff points out that Merwin's work seems innovative and shocking only to amnesiac readers: "Merwin's free verse, which may have seemed enormously innovative when read against the background of the formalism of the fifties—the mode, say, of Richard Wilbur or Allen Tate or Howard Nemerov—was nowhere as explosive as the free verse Pound and Williams were writing by 1916, a free-verse model carried on by Louis Zukofsky and George Oppen in the thirties, and by Charles Olson in the late forties and early fifties" (238). Moreover, "it should have struck the critics as slightly odd that a poetry so seemingly explosive—the poetry of 'the wilderness of unopened life'— was routinely published in the *New Yorker, Poetry*, the *Hudson Review*, and *Harper's*—hardly the organs of the avant-garde" (238).

In *Poetic License* Perloff offers some general formulations concerning the responsibilities of the critic of contemporary poetry. One might assume that her sympathies would lie with an ideologically or theoretically motivated criticism that would lead a critic to claim that "our role as critics is, in the first place, to characterize the dominant discourse and then to read against it that writing it has excluded or marginalized, thus redefining the canon so as to give pride of place to the hitherto repressed" (2). But Perloff rejects such a position, and her critique has important implications for pluralist and multiculturalist perspectives: "Ironically, this [ideologically motivated] stance toward poetry turns out, at least in practice, to be just as essentialist as the first. For in automatically privileging, say, the poetry of women of color over the poetry of white men, we imply that the former are, by definition, more 'sensitive,' more 'authentic,' and, in any case, more 'interesting' than the latter" (2). Perloff proposes that "the impasse of this particular version of a cultural poetics might, I think, be avoided by redefining the term *dominant class* as what Charles Bernstein has called 'official verse culture'" (3). The political implications of style (and a style's relationship to dominant institutional practices of poetry) cut across a vast range of subject positions.

Perloff attacks a pluralism based on message-oriented, ideologically "correct" poetry and sides with McCaffery, who "stresses the need to free poetic language from the co-option by what he calls the 'media model,' the model of 'linguistic transparency' and grammatical rule" (294). At her most exasperated with a poetry of sincerity and clarity, Perloff asks, "if 'poetry' is really no more than . . . straight-but-sensitive 'nuts and bolts' talk broken arbitrarily into line segments so as to remind us that, yes, this is a poem, why read in the first place rather than turning on the TV?" (305). If the new poetry of protest is judged by its message rather than its medium, then "what can it mean to be a critic or literary historian if one does not choose between available alternatives? . . . And how far can we extend the helping hand of 'pluralism' and 'diversity' without making *poetry* so reductive and bland a term that its potential readership merely loses interest?" (35, 36). Perloff's own choice is clear: she sides with a poetry that expresses "the rights of the signifier." (But such an affiliation does not prevent her, in *Poetic License*, from doing sound, thorough writing on Lawrence, Ginsberg, Plath, Paul Blackburn, and others who do not fall readily into the camp of the avant-garde.) She expresses frustration with an academicism that is receptive to poststructuralist criticism but that misapplies that reading to inapplicable strains of contemporary American poetry, "the irony being that the poems of a Charles Bernstein or a Lyn Hejinian, not to speak of Leiris or Cage, are much more consonant with the theories of Derrida and de Man, Lacan and Lyotard, Barthes and Benjamin, than are the canonical texts that are currently being ground through the post-structuralist mill" (23).

Perloff is willing—and here her kindred historian is Sayre—to call into question, fundamentally, where and what a poem is. Her extensive and sympathetic reading of Barthes leads her to claim (over and against Jonathan Culler's reading) "that Barthes's skepticism about 'The Poem' is itself historically determined, that what Barthes is telling us . . . is that perhaps the 'poetic,' in our time, is to be found, not in the conventionally isolated lyric poem, so dear to the Romantics and Symbolists, but in texts not immediately recognizable as poetry" (18).

Though poetry per se plays only a relatively small role in Henry Sayre's (1989) *The Object of Performance: The American Avant-Garde Since 1970*, I can think of no better book to juxtapose with an analysis of contemporary American poetry. In contrast to more conservatively genre-bound and claustrophobic studies, Sayre's book illuminates the options and milieus available to poesis. He warns us that "the medium of avant-garde art is itself 'undecidable,' almost by definition interdisciplinary" (xiii). Sayre begins his introduction with an epigraph from Adorno: "Today the only works which really count are those which are no longer works at all." Sayre's book is stimulating precisely because he "reads" works of art that *do* call into question the nature, location, circulation, and presence of the work of art itself. His book is anything but new wine for old bottles. The bottle itself, the liquor store, and the winery are, if not reinvented, subjected to considerable scrutiny and imagination.

One result is that Sayre does some of the most interesting thinking we have on the commodity status of the work of art. From a perspective similar to Hartley's analysis of reification and the resistance to commodification in the work of the Language poets, Sayre argues that "performance and performance-oriented genres could be defined as artistic strategies conceived—like conceptual art itself—in order to defeat, or at least mitigate, the exploitation of their material manifestations" (12–13). In discussing the earthworks of Smithson, Oppenheim, and others, Sayre cites Oppenheim's observation that "one of the principal functions of artistic involvement is to stretch the limits of what can be done and to show others that art isn't just making objects to put in galleries" (213). By extension, neither is a poem just for putting in an anthology or in a forty-eight- to sixty-four-page collection of thematically unified lyrics. Thus Sayre provides us with a sympathetic context for considering writings that question habitual and institutionalized locations of "the poem."

Sayre links his consideration of resistances to the art object as commodity to his investigation of representations of the self and is at his best in analyzing the implications of the work of certain contemporary photographers. For Garry Winogrand's photographs—in a comment that would be equally astute and helpful in reading much of Perelman's poetry—Sayre suggests, "It is as if the structural harmonies of his scenes were poses beneath which other more complicated and chaotic narrations are unfolding" (47). Or, in thinking about Nicholas Nixon's family portraits, Sayre asks us to consider that "what seems staged or dramatic in one age, then, appears natural to the next, and vice versa, but the point, surely, is that this tension between the natural and the staged seems endemic to the portrait genre as a whole" (49). Sayre concludes, in part by way of exploring William Wegman's photographs, that "the self, finally, is a kind of theater, an ongoing transference of identity, an endless 'acting out' " (57).

Such an observation allows Sayre to offer some interesting insights into the extreme and artificial gestures of self-representation present in punk: "[M]asking oneself up is *revealed* here as a signifying *process*. That is, it creates meaning, and it creates it as a function of *difference*. . . . [P]unk exposes the signifying process of the cosmetics industry—of glamour and style—by radicalizing and literalizing its conventions. It is possible to say, in fact, that punk is 'excessively' conventional, that it is glamour *in excess*" (85). Thus from significantly different objects of attention, Sayre makes an essential contribution to current understandings of the self as an artificial, constructed entity. So, too, does he critique the notion of the autonomous artist working in heroic isolation. In an excellent chapter on feminist art of the seventies, Sayre observes that "feminist art offered collaborative activity as not only an alternative to but a specific critique of the traditional modes of isolated, individually motivated artistic production accepted as the norm in Western culture" (101).

Like Perloff's *Poetic License*, Sayre's *Object of Performance* offers a series of challenges to contemporary poetry's norm of the expressive lyric. One of the most significant challenges to such a conception of the poem is the talk-poem of Antin. As distinguished from the oral poetics movement's reversal of the writing/speech hierarchy, "rather than privileging speech or writing, Antin problematizes their interaction" (210). His talk-poems exist both as live presentations and as written texts produced, with revision, from tape recordings of his performances. But what Antin's work, and Rothenberg's, and indeed much of the artwork discussed throughout Sayre's book, have in common is an assumption that "art is the act of making, not the thing made" (183). Taken collectively, and considered with some seriousness, the wide range of art examined by Sayre should help to undermine restrictive models for an institutionally sanctioned version of "poetry."

So might *A Gift of Tongues: Critical Challenges in Contemporary American Poetry* (1987) and *An Ear to the Ground: An Anthology of Contemporary American Poetry* (1989), both edited by Marie Harris and Kathleen Aguero, help to disturb the institutional practice of poetry. In spite of differences with their approach, I state unequivocally that these books are excellent, informative, and valuable, particularly at a time when teachers, poets, and critics are attempting to imagine and enact multicultural approaches to "American" writing.

In *Ear*, Harris and Aguero (1989) aim for a literature of inclusion: "*An Ear to the Ground* . . . affirms the richness and cultural complexity of contemporary poetry in the United States" and "abandons the myopic notion of center (European, male literary tradition) and periphery (all other cultural influences) in favor of the more accurate representation of contemporary U.S. literature" (xix). P. J. Laska, echoing arguments made several years ago by Ron Silliman, argues that a chief feature of contemporary poetry is its radical decentralization: "Those who lament the passing of the old order talk about the seventies as a 'decade of dispersal' and argue, for example, that Robert Lowell is the last of the great American poets because of the scattering of cultural focus and the fracturing of national audience" (in Harris and Aguero 1987, 324). Laska's decentralized art world, resisted by the McClatchys and the Vendlers, verges on a statement of fact, with significant consequences and options.

One such option is the multiculturalism advocated by Harris and Aguero. While no anthology can include "everything" at any given moment, their attempt to be broadly inclusive in a fresh and provocative way is of great worth. Harris and Aguero (1989) acknowledge that their "own backgrounds and education have not been without bias" (xxii). And there are instances of definite bias and confusion, the most serious of which is the nearly total exclusion, in poems and essays, of any representation of avant-garde poetries. The basis for that particular bias can be seen in the conclusion to the preface to *Tongues* (1987): "If it is true that the poet speaks to everyone, it is essential that the listener not hear selectively, responding only to the familiar voice, the expected message. Poets have a gift of tongues. It is our responsibility and delight to hear them when they speak" (x). Perhaps their bias against experimental writing stems from a valuing of voice over text, a privileging of speech over the productions of the page, a bias that leaves no room for Darragh, or Bernstein, or Martin, or Larry Eigner, or Reyes Cárdenas, or, at another extreme, the talk-poems of Antin, or the radical (textual) feminism of DuPlessis.

A secondary confusion apparent from the conclusion to the preface to *Tongues* (1987) lies in the assumption that "the poet speaks to everyone." These two books emphatically make out the opposite case. Poets speak (or write) from, within, and often to specific audiences. Our job as readers may be to expand the range of poets (and human beings) to which we respond and attend. Indeed, encounters with poems that do not speak to "us" may well provide "us" with one of poetry's most crucial acts of education. Rather than Frost's transcendental category of education by poetry (meaning education by metaphor), we may begin to have an education by difference, especially differences of culture, context, aesthetic assumptions, audience, and subject position. Rather than an ever-expanding canon of ever-broadening inclusivity, the more effective strategy may prove to be Silliman's rejection of the process of canonization itself.

While the Harris and Aguero books reveal some of the pitfalls and difficulties of a multicultural approach to contemporary American poetry — particularly some of the essentialisms that haunt the conception of poetry (and subjectivity) from various subject positions — their books solidly contribute to any serious consideration of contemporary American poetry. *Tongues* (1987), which provides an excellent bibliography of publishers, journals, and anthologies, as well as informative notes at the end of each essay, includes fine essays on poetry by women of color, issues of caste and canon, radical poetries of the thirties, feminist poetry, black poetry, multicultural criticism, Native American poetry, Chicano poetry, Asian-American poetry, Puerto Rican poetry in the United States, gay poetry, poetry in American prisons, and Appalachian poetry. Several of the most important specific contributions in *Tongues* are Adrian Oktenberg's introduction to the poetry of Meridel Le Sueur, John Crawford's writing on Lorna Dee Cervantes' *Emplumada*, Joseph Bruchac's "Contemporary Native American Poetry," and Carmen Tafolla's important "Chicano Literature: Beyond Beginnings."

Where Perloff (1990) objects in *Poetic License* to a reverse prejudice (that values "message" over form) in the evaluation of poetry, Tafolla, by means of numerous examples, provides the most sustained instance I have encountered of writing on "ethnic" poetry noteworthy for its innovations (rather than its imitation of or adherence to a reigning professional version of "good writing"). He cites the work of Alurista (particularly *Spik in Glyph?*) and Cárdenas. I offer an extended paragraph of examples cited by Tafolla to give the reader an idea of the innovations available in contemporary Chicano poetry:

> Regional chauvinists continued to criticize our "Tex-Mex" and to treat it as a "language deficiency" caused by low educational or intellectual levels. And Chicano writers continued to indulge in "language play" (for example, Nephtalí de León's play *Tequila Mockingbird* and Alurista's *Spik in Glyph?*), an inventive and intriguing challenge for linguistic creativity. What had begun with reflections of our own bilingual reality—my own *"me senté allí en la English class"* and Delgado's "chicotazos of history"—turned into the formulation of totally new grammatical styles. Lexical creations spring from the discovery of new worlds of thought and literature—the Mayan, Aztec, Native American, and so forth. Formerly we would, in our daily lives, hispanicize English realities: "I missed" would resurrect in Spanish as *"mistié,"* "I flunked" would expand the traditional lexicon with *"flonquié,"* and the "big, old thing" ending *"azo"* would turn a party in an English sentence into a *porazo* in a Spanish conversation. . . . Acutely aware of the sounds of English, we would accent our Spanish to a mock-Anglicized "free holes" (for *frijoles*) and then play the reverse by accenting our English with the sounds of Spanish: *pino borra* for "peanut butter." Now, reading through Aztec accounts of *teotl, mitotl, coatl, tomatl*, we exclaimed, instead of the commonplace "¡Qué loco!" ("Crazy!"), "¡Qué locotl!" And the new *mestizaje* of language yielded concentrated high-impact packs, like the three-word label of the moon by Victoria Moreno—"vanilla, canela crescent." (in *Tongues* 208–9)

For such language play, Juan Bruce-Novoa introduces the descriptive term "interlingual." Such examples, as well as Tafolla's claim for a third stage of development in Chicano literature—"a stage of invention and creation" (223) succeeding a statement of protest—makes his introduction to contemporary Chicano writing one of the most exciting essays in the books edited by Harris and Aguero.

There are several essays in *Tongues* I shall explore in greater detail, particularly to illustrate dangers present in today's first approaches to a multicultural contemporary American poetry. Lynda Koolish's "The Bones of This Body Say, Dance: Self-Empowerment in Contemporary Poetry by Women of Color" offers a statement of goals for women writers that is, by now, relatively standard: "The woman writer in this culture—whether Afro-American, Chicana, Asian American, Native American, or white—has written in a language determined by patriarchy as well as racism and thus has a double urgency to redefine that language, to claim a language and form unfettered by those twin forces of the dominant culture" (*Tongues* 13). When discussing the dilemmas facing Asian-American and Chicana poets, Koolish is sensitive to the dangers of assimilation and standardization: "The paradox here, of course, is that in 'translating oneself into understandable terms' the North American woman of color whose native tongue is not English runs the risk of being increasingly understandable to the Anglo world while becoming increasingly alienated from her own identity" (19). Even so, Koolish praises Audre Lorde for poems of "immediate, unmediated description" and "tremendous impact," poems that catch the reader up in visceral experience (6). Koolish exalts certain poems because "poetry makes the unknowable intelligible." She claims that "in Native American poetry . . . access is provided to the mysterious and creative powers of the universe and thus to one's own inner power" (43). Joy Harjo's poems allow the reader "to become one with the earth" (43). From another poem, we learn that "memory restores us to ourselves" (46).

What worries me is the mixture of easy aestheticism and an unquestioned faith in humanist platitudes and individual autonomy. Formally, a more subtle threat exists to the "difference" from which Koolish's poets write. The threat of standardization, under the banner of "excellence," derives from a homogenized version of professionalized verse practice: a contemporary academicism of the workshop, a poetry of an "autonomous" individual voice that fails to investigate the rhetorical underpinnings of its stylized and (bourgeois) ideological practice.

Such criticism does not apply only to Koolish's essay. Crawford, in "Toward a New Multicultural Criticism," praises Cervantes's poems because, among other virtues, "she speaks in her own voice" (*Tongues* 171). The conclusion to Crawford's essay is especially noteworthy:

The common element of their [Joy Harjo's, Lorna Dee Cervantes's, and Janice Mirikatani's] work, after all, is that it is different from the poetry of the dominant Anglo-American culture which represents the

aspirations and interests of the majority of the population of the United
States (if we are to count the assimilated white ethnic minorities). All
then that we can generalize about is the *difference* of this work, which
sees its project in diverse ways as one of rescuing images from the dominant culture, restoring a sense of rightness in a threatened social and
personal world, and proposing a means of continuing to exist—and to
struggle—in the future. (*Tongues* 192)

Not the least of the many problems with such an assessment is that a key
portion of this passage—the last sentence—would serve equally well as
a blurb for the mainstream poetry of white males such as Gerald Stern,
Philip Levine, or any one of a number of other popular poets of personal
struggle. The problem is that for Crawford, Koolish, and many other critics there is already in place an uncontested version of "good writing,"
which I think of as a kind of homogenized academicism. Along with its
considerable virtues, *Ear* presents many poems that give ample evidence
that the voice-poem, of clear simple imagery with heightened emotion and
a moment of revelation/closure, is indeed a virus that has migrated from
one cultural site to another.

In the latter portions of Juan Bruce-Novoa's essay in *Tongues*, he calls
attention to what he considers to be the best of recent Chicano poetry (a
list considerably at odds with Tafolla's more adventurous readings). The
terms of Bruce-Novoa's praise provide one more instance of contemporary
poetry's homogenized professionalization. He acclaims the work of Gary
Soto (who studied under Levine) and Cervantes for producing "a series
of publications that for the most part demanded craft before message"
and that "displayed attention to technique" (243). Throughout the last few
pages of Bruce-Novoa's essay, this word "craft" pops up again and again.
Soto's poems are praised for "craft"—"tight poems based more on image
and metaphor than on narrative anecdote" (244)—and for "the quality of
his work [that] has set a standard that continues to serve others as a bench-
mark" (244).

But what version of "craft" and "quality" is being praised? Bruce-Novoa
is reasonably clear on this point: a version learned from the academic
mainstream, that is, the workshop voice-poem, the lyric of personal experience stated in "natural," clear language. Bruce-Novoa's trinity is "crafts-
manship, quality, and dedication to a personal vision" (244). Cervantes
thus is praised for poems worked on "until each word fits perfectly" and
for the display of "brilliant images" (245).

Bruce-Novoa's vision of contemporary Chicano poetry, considerably different from Tafolla's, is that "Chicano poets are less concerned with ideology and more with craft; they explore the personal voice in any register and through any technique" (246). But any version of "craft" *is* ideological, particularly today's mainstream craft which makes "the personal voice" the essential product of an accomplished poet. Bruce-Novoa argues that the emergence of craft over message "makes the recent [Chicano] poetry . . . more dynamic, healthy, and interesting" (246). I claim that a poetic culture is "dynamic, healthy, and interesting" when it is oppositional and innovative, not when it is assimilating an already outmoded, conservative poetics of the personal voice. Admittedly, money, power, and prestige may result from such acts of "craft," but at the expense of "difference." The ironically conventional formal character of much that Bruce-Novoa celebrates in Chicano poetry illustrates a serious difficulty in the effort to claim a subject position for a previously marginalized other. That effort may easily fall prey to the lures of appropriation. To state the problem in general terms, the valid need that some poetry work for the construction of communities may be mistakenly conceived as depending on conventions of literary subjectivity borrowed (or appropriated) from the dominant culture, so that a resistance to appropriation may give way to a politics of assimilation. It seems to me that Bruce-Novoa's chief error is to pretend that "craft" is not ideological or institutional in nature. He writes as if "craft" were itself a transcendent, ahistorical accomplishment. The exact opposite is the case, particularly for the version of "craft" he endorses.

The same holds true for Bruchac's conclusions regarding poems written by prisoners. Bruchac concludes:

> Some continue to view the work of writers in prison as little more than a literary curiosity, despite the fact that much of the current poetry from prisons is moving and highly crafted, despite the fact that a large part of the poetic output of American inmates makes no mention of prison and is being published because of its excellence, not its origin. The only fair way to judge the work produced by that varied community of men and women in our nation who have been legally defined as outcasts is to use the same criteria you use to judge all good writing. (*Tongues* 294)

But what both *Ear* and *Tongues* and the entire project of multiculturalism teach us is the opposite. In fact, judgment is not the issue, for judgment (as Paul Lauter, Silliman, and others argue) is simply a result of critical method. The issue, says Lauter, is not " 'better,' but what we mean by 'better'"(*Tongues* 66). As Harris and Aguero themselves stipulate in the preface to *Ear*, "we need the opportunity to abandon narrow definitions and limiting assumptions and evaluate the poem from the inside out without comparing one tradition to another or judging against an artificially imposed single standard" (xxii).

The lessons of multiculturalism are varied, but we can begin to assert that subject position and context *do* matter. We cannot, therefore, use the same "commonsense" standards of excellence to evaluate poetries written out of radically different traditions. As Perloff (1990), Hartley (1989), and Bernstein (1990) demonstrate, definitions of "craft" and "quality" are ideological and are part of cultural and institutional struggles. If poetry is to retain (or return to) a place of importance and excitement, poets must engage in an oppositional practice of form *and* content inseparably. Not just "make it new" for the sake of a commodified novelty, but make it new so that the writing of poetry continues to be radically exploratory, not merely learning how to do what the currently entrenched do.

5. Experimentation and Politics

Contemporary Poetry as Commodity

I am out of my element.[1] I don't really know your business, but I also do not think that it is none of my business. I write books, read books, write about books, I buy books, talk about books, check out books, and I check into books. I want today to think with you about books; I hope to do so in a manner at once theoretical and practical, unabashedly partial and partially informative.

While I do wish to think of your work in economic and social terms, from the outset I also wish to make clear that I am *not* talking about the entire range of your economic activity. I am thinking of a small portion of your activity, but nevertheless a domain within which you already do have a significant impact. That is, my essay attends to your relationship to books of contemporary American poetry. I am further limiting my remarks to what you might call a small discretionary portion of your purchasing budget.

Ron Silliman (1987) claims in the provocative opening sentence of an essay called "The Political Economy of Poetry" that "poems both are and are not commodities" (20). While much of my activity as poet and teacher is spent exploring the ways in which poems may *resist* commodification while they participate in and inform a socialized resistance to authority, today I wish to think more earnestly about poems, and especially books of poems, as commodities. Thought of (somewhat inaccurately) as a collective body, libraries (and universities) have great impact on the survival, audibility, sanctioning, and circulation of books of poetry. I fear that the purchasing habits of libraries contribute significantly to the impoverishment of contemporary American poetry. Through a very blurred decision-making process, it is easy to reinforce a tragically narrowed and narrowing version of contemporary American poetry. Acquisition, circulation, visibility, and availability all are forms of sanctioning and investing in (or denying investment in) the vitality of a press; the decision *not* to purchase a particular book of poems, individually willed or passed along to a more distanced agent under the name of necessity or efficiency, is in effect a decision to silence. It is easy to imagine a pattern of purchasing in which certain varieties of expression are, in effect, censored. Even (or especially?) the "genteel" and "sensitive" world of poetry involves struggle and violence. Each survival and enshrinement of a body of work involves the erasure of another. Silliman argues, "public canons disempower readers and disappear poets. They are conscious acts of violence" (in Bernstein 1990, 153).

Through timidity and ignorance, compounded by underfunding and a consequent understaffing, university libraries may participate in a conservative, self-defeating perpetuation of mainstream poetry's hegemony and intellectual irrelevance. Admittedly, the economic and numerical situation for contemporary American poetry is a bit overwhelming. Dana Gioia (May 1991) outlines that situation in his provocative essay "Can Poetry Matter?"

> The proliferation of new poetry and poetry programs is astounding by any historical measure. Just under a thousand new collections of verse are published each year, in addition to a myriad of new poems printed in magazines both small and large. No one knows how many poetry readings take place each year, but surely the total must run into the tens of thousands. And there are now about 200 graduate creative-writing programs in the United States, and more than a thousand undergraduate ones. With an average of ten poetry students in each graduate section, these programs alone will produce about 20,000 accredited professional poets over the next decade. From such statistics an observer might easily conclude that we live in the golden age of American poetry.
>
> But the poetry boom has been a distressingly confined phenomenon. Decades of public and private funding have created a large professional class for the production and reception of new poetry, comprising legions of teachers, graduate students, editors, publishers, and administrators. Based mostly in universities, these groups have gradually be-

come the primary audience for contemporary verse. Consequently, the energy of American poetry, which once was directed outward, is now increasingly focused inward. Reputations are made and rewards distributed within the poetry subculture. To adapt Russell Jacoby's definition of contemporary academic renown from *The Last Intellectuals*, a "famous" poet now means someone famous only to other poets. But there are enough poets to make that local fame relatively meaningful. Not long ago, "only poets read poetry" was meant as damning criticism. Now it is a proven marketing strategy.

The situation has become a paradox, a Zen riddle of cultural sociology. Over the past half century, as American poetry's specialist audience has steadily expanded, its general readership has declined. Moreover, the engines that have driven poetry's institutional success—the explosion of academic writing programs, the proliferation of subsidized magazines and presses, the emergence of a creative-writing career track, and migration of American literary culture to the university—have unwittingly contributed to its disappearance from public view. (95)

What are librarians to do in such an environment?

Serve poetry and the book, *not* the university and its own often narrowly conceived and self-serving forms of professionalism. That is, library staff members with purchasing authority must adopt a more skeptical, informed, investigative relationship to the social, political, and economic ramifications of their habits as poetry-consumers.

I believe libraries currently cooperate with a conservative, misplaced hierarchy of values by overvaluing the importance of "reputable" publication sources: trade presses and university presses. As Ron Silliman (1987) argues, the "alliance [of trade presses] with capital yields another major advantage: the relative efficiency of trade distribution virtually guarantees its predominance on college course reading lists, *which is the largest single market for books of poetry*, with 2500 colleges and 200 writing programs in North America" (30). As Silliman (1990) points out in his essay "Canons and Institutions: New Hope for the Disappeared,"

The primary institution of American poetry is the university. In addition to its own practices, it provides important mediation and legitimation functions for virtually every other social apparatus that relates publically to the poem. The university provides the context in which many, and perhaps most, poetry readers are first introduced to the writing of our time; it may even be, as has sometimes been argued, the context in which the majority of all poems in the U.S. are both written and read. (157)

Charles Bernstein's (1986) term for the dominant institutional network for poetry is official verse culture, which he defines and decries as follows:

Let me be specific as to what I mean by "official verse culture" — I am referring to the poetry publishing and reviewing practices of *The New York Times*, *The Nation*, *American Poetry Review*, *The New York Review of Books*, *The New Yorker*, *Poetry* (Chicago), *Antaeus*, *Parnassus*, Atheneum Press, all the major trade publishers, the poetry series of almost all of the major university presses (the University of California Press being a significant exception at present). Add to this the ideologically motivated selection of the vast majority of poets teaching in university writing and literature programs and of poets taught in such programs as well as the interlocking accreditation of these selections through prizes and awards judged by these same individuals. Finally, there are the self-appointed keepers of the gate who actively put forward biased, narrowly focussed and frequently shrill and contentious accounts of American poetry, while claiming, like all disinformation propaganda, to be giving historical or nonpartisan views. In this category, the American Academy of Poetry and such books as *The Harvard Guide to Contemporary American Writing* stand out. . . . What makes official verse culture official is that it denies the ideological nature of its practice while maintaining hegemony in terms of major media exposure and academic legitimation and funding. (247–49)

I enjoy thinking about Wallace Stevens' "Large Red Man Reading," who "sat there reading, from out of the purple tabulae, / The outlines of being and its expressings, the syllables of its law: / *Poesis, poesis*, the literal characters, the vatic lines" (320). I am drawn as well to Edmond Jabès's suggestion in *The Book of Questions*: " 'The man crazy about writing dreams of being a shadow in order to marry the water. From this union, books are born' " (77). But it is too easy for such lines of investigation, especially for one such as myself who is situated within an academic setting (and has been for a long time), to be a self-serving form of blindness to the material and social circumstances of poetry's production and reception. In "Poetry's Institutional Settings," the insightful opening chapter of his book *Languages of Liberation: The Social Text in Contemporary American Poetry*, Walter Kalaidjian (1989) argues,

Today, poetry's pastoral valley resembles less a "sacred wood" than a resort condo community. In fact, much executive tampering enters into the decisions about where and under what circumstances poets will be published, what awards will accrue to them, which organizations and performing circuits will underwrite their public readings, and how critics will cultivate their audiences. Verse writing in the postmodern era, it is plausible to claim, is less a visionary or sacramental art than a highly competitive industry. (15)

Poetry's institutional setting, wrapped in the gauze of humanistic platitudes and content-oriented thematic studies of poetry, leaves us blind to poetry as business. To reiterate: poems are, partially, commodities.

Kalaidjian offers an interesting, if alarming, narrative of the broader publishing environment in which poetry has its small toehold (or in which poetry is held as a cute cultural adornment). He begins with Bennett Cerf's speech in 1960 to the New York Society of Security Analysts. Cerf, then president of Random House, envisioned a publishing scene, like the steel and automobile industries, which would be dominated by five or six great publishing combines; Cerf wanted to be sure that Random House would be one of those giants. What he did not foresee was the broader form of industrial mergers in the 1980s. Random House, for example, was taken over by RCA, the parent company of NBC. Kalaidjian continues:

Even more disturbing, by 1982 five parent companies owned half of the mass publishing market, while the top ten managed 85 percent. Merger mania in the 1980s was fostered by the relaxed antitrust atmosphere of the Reagan White House. Such domestic mergers, coupled with a weakening U.S. dollar, fueled foreign investments in the lucrative $10 billion American book sales market. In 1986, for example, the West German communications giant Bertelsmann bought Doubleday and Company for $500 million, making it the second largest book publisher after Simon and Schuster. Other European entities such as the Holtzbrinck Group, Elsevier, and Penguin Books of Britain have taken over Henry Holt and Company, Praeger, New American Library, Viking, and E.P. Dutton.

In addition to their holdings in industrial and manufacturing economies, giant conglomerates such as Time, Gulf + Western, CBS, MCA, Times Mirror, and Westinghouse wholly control the diversified sectors of America's mass culture industry. . . . As Time demonstrates in the conglomerate market, the distinction between private ownership of mass communications networks and their "objective" content is blurred. As the mass media is increasingly bureaucratized and centered in a literal handful of giant service conglomerates, the likelihood of a diverse, heterogeneous national culture grows increasingly remote.

Contemporary poets, as a result, are fated to write either for an audience largely oriented to the homogeneous representations of a monolithic culture industry or for fringe readerships pushed to the edge of America's cultural scene. But more troubling, poets live with the reality that they are bought and sold by the same conglomerates that marginalize their art. Resisting the mass publishing market, many poets start up their own small presses and alternative magazines, often moving into desk-top publishing through the laborsaving advances of laser printing and computer technology. (16–18)

Libraries ought to support actively these moves toward greater autonomy and decentralization. You cannot buy *all* books, even of poetry. With your admittedly limited resources, *which* books will you house? Which books—produced within what sorts of social formations, selected by what standards of judgment, and manufactured by what kinds of labor —will you legitimate? Approval plans are aptly named. Purchases amount to tacit forms of approval, sanctioning and ensuring the availability of certain kinds of poetry and certain approved authors whose channels of publication meet with approval.

When we consider that press runs today for poetry are usually between 400 and 1,000 copies, your purchasing habits matter.[2] We should also remember that (relatively recent) tax and warehousing regulations slide many poetry books quickly toward remainder stands ("reduced for quick sale") and shredders. The window of opportunity for purchasing a book of poetry has become a relatively narrow one.

I would urge you to consider, collectively, reversing what may currently be a library's pyramid of buying practices for primary texts of contemporary American poetry. Rather than the broad base of nearly automatic purchase of books by trade and university presses, and, on a very selective basis the purchase of a few experimental and small press books, reverse that pyramid. Trade books will be purchased often enough by libraries anyway (including many public libraries) to ensure their ready, perpetual availability. Knowing that any purchase activates the dynamics of approval and disapproval, legitimation and denial, audibility and silence, why support automatically the formation and methods of concentrated capital?

Why purchase, automatically, the products of a corporate conglomerate whose principal loyalties are to profit-making in movies and other forms of mass communication? Why would you expect or assume that such an entity will do a good job of knowing, judging, and publishing poetry? Are theirs the versions of poetry you wish to subsidize and perpetuate? Won't such enterprises sometimes decide that it is inefficient to assign and pay a full-time poetry editor when it is easier and more cost-effective to combine responsibilities by assigning the poetry duties to the cookbook editor?[3]

I do not wish to be so simplistic as to claim that if a book of poems is published by a press associated with a large communications conglomerate that the poetry is bad. I know that there are many examples that counter such an argument; indeed, I read and teach many such books with pleasure. Nevertheless, a sustained consideration of poetry's economic and social dimensions resituates and alters arguments over value, excellence, and especially politics in poetry.

I share Ron Silliman's call for a rethinking and revitalizing of poetry's institutional setting. Silliman (1990) suggests,

> Redirecting creative writing programs toward poetics, for example, will require a breakdown of massive amounts of hardened institutional inertia. . . . A pluralization of the poetry publishing programs of university presses—a level of the academy that is even more arthritic and senile than MFA programs—will have to begin with the delegitimation of what is presently being done. That the preservation of the work of poets such as Lew Welch, Jack Spicer, and Paul Blackburn has fallen entirely into the hands of independent small publishers constitutes a fundamental refusal of responsibility on the part of the state. This is not to suggest that the conservative-to-reactionary poetry programs of such schools as Pittsburgh, Wesleyan, Princeton, and Yale should not exist, but that they must be contextualized in terms of the failure of these schools and others to present the full range of what has been written in recent American history. (169)

My suggestion today is that the research library has an important role to play in this struggle for redefinition.

In spite of the ardor of my argument, one might still ask, why be so concerned with what takes place in a minuscule corner of the book market? Because essential issues of freedom, labor, resistance, and meaning-making are at stake. Because these textual relations enact and rhyme with broader, more general social and political relations. In "What Are Poets For?" Heidegger (1971) tells us that "language is the house of Being; we reach what is by constantly going through this house" (132). But a more chilling and commercially apt view of that neighborhood is Raymond Williams's (1977) observation that " 'Freedom to publish,' for example, can be practically redefined as 'freedom to publish at a profit' " (200). We don't need state censorship when economic imperatives, in an interlocking system of legitimation in which libraries may unwittingly be complicit, are sufficient to silence or sufficiently discredit alternative or noninstrumental explorations of and in language (see, for example, Coffey, 23 November 1990). Raymond Williams (1977) concludes,

> real social relations are deeply embedded within the practice of writing itself, as well as in the relations within which writing is read. To write in different ways is to live in different ways. It is also to be read in different ways, in different relations, and often by different people. This area of possibility, and thence of choice, is specific, not abstract, and commitment in its only important sense is specific in just these terms. (205)

In thinking about the disappearance from public access of the writing of poets such as Joseph Ceravolo and Lew Welch, Ron Silliman (1990) offers some disturbing reflections:

> I am haunted by such disappearances as these from the public discourse and consciousness of poetry not only because of the manifest unfairness that results when the hard-earned labors of fine artists goes unnoticed and unrewarded, but because poetry itself is impoverished whenever and wherever its rich and diverse roots atrophy. A poetry without history strikes me as bordering on the unintelligible, its social value, its very use to us in our daily lives, seems to me questionable, and its fate a mere choice between oblivion and the still worse doom of perpetually repeating itself. Yet instances of literary forgetfulness such as these— and I could speak for days simply listing others—indicate that poetry, particularly in the United States, is a profoundly amnesiac discourse. The stereotypic figure of the artist unrecognized in her or his own time who emerges decades or centuries later to become one of the building blocks of western civilization is really the reverse side of a more ominous token: our society discards enormous quantities of that which it could benefit from, and this includes poetry. The shelf life of a good poet may be something less than the half-life of a styrofoam cup.
>
> So I discover that in this sense I'm a conservative: I want to pre-

serve the heritage that I believe American poetry can offer to writers and readers today. A heritage that I find to be both troubled and fragile in much the same way that America's wilderness is troubled and fragile, for the public disappearance of the work of a decent poet is not too terribly different from the extinction of a species in the wild. (150)

It is critical that libraries too stake their limited resources on this utopian project of textual ecology.[4]

The need for multicultural diversity in library collections (and everywhere else, such as in syllabi, course offerings, anthologies, and faculty hiring decisions) is already reasonably well understood (though by no means fully accomplished). But I believe that the issue of poetic form is every bit as *fundamentally* important as multicultural diversity and also every bit as much the arena for xenophobic institutional discrimination (see Chapter 3). As I have argued elsewhere, it is easy to incorporate and sanction forms of multicultural poetic expression that, to a large degree, replicate mainstream poetry's formal constraints and, of greater importance, outmoded versions of subjectivity (see Chapter 4). I agree with Charles Bernstein's (1990) insistence "that stylistic innovations be recognized not only as alternative aesthetic conventions but also as alternative social formations" (242).

Perhaps the principal value of innovative poetries is the putting into question of relations that are too often thought (or not thought and therefore assumed) to be "natural" or given or already understood. The very difficulty and unfamiliarity of such work brings about, of necessity, a collaborative and less certain relationship between reader and writer, or between reader and book. If we insist, in poetry, on "clear" writing that offers "memorable" and "moving" "personal" expression in a "distinctive voice," we abdicate the best and most adventurous exploratory functions, as well as the most radical political deeds, of poetry. It is all too easy to forget that "clear" expository writing itself is a historical (and not a transcendental) form of "correctness." Charles Bernstein (1986) claims,

> as a mode, contemporary expository writing edges close to being merely a *style* of decorous thinking, rigidified and formalized to a point severed from its historical relation to method in Descartes and Bacon. It is no longer an enactment of thinking or reasoning but a representation (and simplification) of an eighteenth-century ideal of reasoning. And yet the hegemony of its practice is rarely questioned outside certain poetic and philosophic contexts. On this level, I would characterize as sharing a

Experimentation and Politics 87

political project both a philosophic practice and a poetic practice that refuse to adopt expository principles as their basic claim to validity.

> For both poetry and philosophy, the order of the elements of a discourse is value constituting and indeed experience engendering, and therefore always at issue, never assumable. (221)

To assume as given the principle of "clear" poetic expression is to give away much of a unique social and political opportunity to reorder our existence. Bernstein (1986) emphasizes writing as a meaning-*making* action:

> Decontextualized codification of the rules of language enforces a view that language operates on principles apart from its usage. . . . The understanding begins to be lost that we are each involved in the constitution of language—that our actions reconstitute—change—reality.
>
> It's a question of who controls reality. Is reality "out there" (as scientism tells us) or rather an interaction with us, in which our actions shape its constitution? Prescribed rules of grammar & spelling make language seem outside of our control. & a language, even only seemingly, wrested from our control is a world taken from us—a world in which language becomes a tool for the description of the world, words mere instrumentalities for representing this world. (26–27)

The writing that I am advocating provides many different forms of resistance to predominantly instrumental and representational uses of language. Such innovative writers, as Gil Ott (1989) suggests in his book of poems *Public Domain*, abstain from the production of "contributory linguistic ornament" (2). Far from being meaningless or antisocial or elitist, such poetry "explicitly holds open the possibility of producing, rather than reproducing, ideas" and explores "how reading and writing can partake of noninstrumental values and thus be utopian formations" (Bernstein 1986, 368, 386).

Particular to such a utopian formation is a radically altered relationship between reader and writer:

> Rather than work which is the product of the "author's" projection/memory/associative process, it [the text] is work for the reader's (viewer's) projection/construction. The text calls upon the reader to be actively involved in the process of constituting its meaning, the reader becoming a neutral observer neither to a described exteriority nor to an enacted interiority. The text formally involves the process of response/interpretation and in so doing makes the reader aware of

herself or himself as producer as well as consumer of meaning. It calls the reader to action, questioning, self-examination: to a reconsideration and remaking of the habits, automatisms, conventions, beliefs through which, and only through which, we see and interpret the world. It insists that there is, in any case, no seeing without interpretation and chooses to incorporate this interpretive process actively by bringing it into view rather than to exploit it passively by deleting its tracks. (Bernstein 1986, 233)

Such thinking shifts the terms of Dana Gioia's (May 1991) lament in "Can Poetry Matter?" Charles Bernstein's (1990) regret "is not the lack of mass audience for any particular poet but the lack of poetic thinking as an activated potential for all people" (241).

I conclude with information about a distribution center for innovative and small press poetry, as well as a few principles to consider. Small Press Distribution 1814 San Pablo Ave., Berkeley, CA 94702.

a. The Best of New Writing. (An individually tailored standing order plan for libraries). At present, only about fifteen libraries are making use of this program
b. Multicultural Series Checklists for African American Books, Native American Books, Asian American Books, and Hispanic Books

Some principles to consider:

1. First, support local and regional experimental writing and small press activity. Don't wait for some external or national mechanism of judgment to validate the writing; your initial support might make possible a sustained consideration of the writing.
2. Emphasize and purchase books that affirm multicultural diversity, but do so of course, with an eye to the particularities of a library's local population as well as the academic emphases of the institution. That is, extensive purchases of Hispanic writing may make more sense in San Jose than in Tuscaloosa.
3. Take risks. Sample the work of many presses. Especially seek out work that seems confusing, unusual, different, adventurous, and irritating.
4. If your funds are not unlimited, select a few presses and writers for particular emphasis (based on readings of catalogs, some exploratory orders, and some other investigative work in sources such as *Small*

Press Magazine, American Book Review, New Pages, and even *Publishers Weekly*).

5. Invite innovative publisher/editors to give talks at your library. The stories they have to tell are of great value; they may point toward the interlocking relationships of economics, politics, and aesthetics. Such talks offer an inexpensive (and at times exciting) way, along with a book display, to publicize and make more coherent a library's holdings, as well as a means to make more tangible to students, faculty, and library staff the material nature of poetry's publication.

6. Thinking Made in the Mouth

The Cultural Poetics of David Antin and Jerome Rothenberg

For at least ten years we have seen a barrage of essays and books lamenting the sad state of contemporary American poetry. In spite of accurate laments—about the sameness of mainstream poetry's product, a lack of intellectual ambition, a narcissistic and limited version of self-expression, the taming effects of poetry's almost absolute institutionalization—such evaluations are almost guaranteed by narrow reading habits and conservative institutional practices that limit the field of consideration.[1] The latest and best of these myopic complaints is Dana Gioia's (1991) argument that in spite of the boom in poetry writing programs, poetry publications in books and magazines, and the proliferation of poetry writing grants, prizes, and readings,

> the energy of American poetry, which once was directed outward, is now increasingly focused inward. . . . Moreover, the engines that have driven poetry's institutional success—the explosion of academic writing programs, the proliferation of subsidized magazines and presses, the emergence of a creative-writing career track, and migration of American literary culture to the university—have unwittingly contributed to its disappearance from public view. (95)

Or, as another recent critic suggests, "Verse writing in the postmodern era . . . is less a visionary or sacramental art than a highly competitive industry" (Kalaidjian 1989, 15).

But such characterizations depend on a limited and limiting exposure to contemporary American poetry. To put it simply, there are many fine, important, and challenging poetries being written today, though most of them are inaudible in mainstream critical analyses, in the models used in creative writing courses, and in the "major" American literature and contemporary poetry anthologies. Cary Nelson (1989) in analyzing the peculiarities of erasure in prevailing histories of modern American poetry, argues that

> indeed, we tend to be unaware of how or why such a process of literary forgetfulness occurs, let alone why it occurs among the very people who consider themselves the custodians of our literary heritage. Custodians, of course, concern themselves not only with conserving the past but also with selectively disposing of much of it, though the two impulses become deceptively conflated in the imagination of academic disciplines—so that a self-congratulatory process of conservation remains primarily in view. (4)

Such remarks apply to current custodial actions with regard to the preservation and presentation of *contemporary* writing as well. The two examples I examine in this essay—the work of David Antin and Jerome Rothenberg—are but two of many that point to the health, intelligence, and range of contemporary poetry. In these two cases, I am dealing with a range of activity that has established itself over the past thirty-five years but whose work is absolutely unrepresented and unacknowledged in the Norton anthology used in most universities, indeed in all other "major" anthologies of American literature and modern poetry.

Perhaps such exclusions can be explained, in part, by developments in academic specializations; that is, in recent disciplinary formations. Over the past thirty years, "creative writing" programs have separated themselves out from "academic" literary programs. Even though most creative writing programs require a substantial component of academic literary courses, already the very distinction contrasts creative writing with other forms of writing. More important, the ideology of most creative writing programs promotes an identity built upon a hostility toward the so-called abstractness of theory. It may also be true that the popularity (and professional necessity) of training in theory has indeed taken away from an interest in contemporary poetry. Such a lack of interest is understandable when the complexity, stylistic adventurousness, and intellectual excitement of many forms of theory are placed beside the too often accepted, but erroneous characterization of contemporary poetry as a somewhat feeble-minded and nostalgic lyricism of outmoded self-expression. I argue that the writings of Antin and Rothenberg (as well as a host of emerging writers such as Charles Bernstein, Susan Howe, Lyn Hejinian, Ron Silliman, Alan Davies, Barrett Watten, and Bruce Andrews) demonstrate convincingly the aberrant and deleterious nature of such institutional disciplinary divisions. Thus the poet/writer who writes in opposition to divisive disciplinary professionalisms, according to Rothenberg, stands in a position similar to that of the native-informant who opposes a distanced version of the anthropologist: "The antagonism to literature and to criticism is, for the poet and artist, no different from that to anthropology, say, on the part of the Native American militant. It is a question in short of the right to self-definition" (Rothenberg 1981, 171).

Antin and Rothenberg, both prolific discursive writers as well as poets, do not reject the value of critical writing and thinking. Indirectly, they critique the institutional separation of those activities and the added implicit claim of professionalized critics to have the right to define the nature of "important" poetry. Rothenberg (1981) proposes "that poetry is not simply what is called 'poetry,' which usually refers to a semi-professional literary activity. I think poetry is involved with the creation of meaning through language. There are a lot of boundaries which get crossed here. Poetry is attempting to discover the otherwise unknowable" (222–23).

Whatever the precise root causes of the institutionalized divisions critiqued by Antin and Rothenberg, we find ourselves in a situation best described by Ron Silliman (1990): "the stereotypic figure of the artist unrecognized in her or his own time who emerges decades or centuries later to become one of the building blocks of western civilization is really the reverse side of a more ominous token: our society discards enormous quantities of that which it could benefit from, and this includes poetry. The shelf life of a good poet may be something less than the half-life of a styrofoam cup" (150). One result is that often "poetry, particularly in the United States, is a *profoundly amnesiac discourse*" (150; my emphasis). Many poets today, with little or no "shelf life," offer important information to us, including the kind of personal guidance and essential pedagogy that is often cited as a function of myth and ritual, namely "educating the imaginative function that must assemble the possibilities for acting" (Doty 1986: 33).

For Jerome Rothenberg (1981) such an assembly begins with an act of conservation and reinhabitation, principally in new anthologies and translations which provide a means of recovery:

> the matters that touch on the "recovery" are, first, the idea of poesis as a primary human process; second, the primacy of the "oral tradition" in poesis; third, the re-invigoration of the bond between ourselves & other living beings; fourth, the exploration of a common ground for "history" & "dream-time" (myth); & fifth, the "re-invention of human liberty" (S. Diamond) in the shadow of the total state. (120)

The activity of recovery, shared by Antin and Rothenberg (who have worked together for some thirty-five years as editors, friends, collaborators, and now as professional/academic colleagues), involves a broadening and inclusive notion of poetry, one that directs us toward sources and disciplines beyond what are conventionally considered to be "literary" and "poetic," including anthropology, archaeology, linguistics, philosophy, and mythography. As one of Rothenberg's (1983) many anthologies has it, we are directed toward a "A Symposium of the Whole" (Rothenberg and Rothenberg 1983).

One aspect of such a project is a radical rethinking of the relationships between the modern and the primitive, a rethinking that causes Rothenberg (1981) to leave "open the question of whether the 'primitive' is influencing the 'modern' or the 'modern' is directing our attention to forms we may now recognize as poems in tribal/oral cultures" (20). Antin's rethinking of the modern undermines our current, glib "postmodern" sense that modernism is somehow distant and finished. In his astonishing essay "Modernism and Postmodernism: Approaching the Present in American Poetry," published some twelve years prior to Fredric Jameson's supposedly seminal essay on postmodernism (and written with a range of understanding of poetry and the visual and plastic arts which puts Jameson to shame), Antin (1972) argues,

> Clearly the sense that such a thing as a "postmodern" sensibility exists and should be defined is wrapped up with the conviction that what we have called "modern" for so long is thoroughly over. If we are capable of imagining the "modern" as a closed set of stylistic features, "modern" can no longer mean present. For it is precisely the distinctive feature of the present that, in spite of any strong sense of its coherence, it is always open on its forward side. (98–99)

Antin (1972) wonders, "when and to whom did the career of 'modern' American poetry appear to be over and what did this mean?" (100). For Antin, and for a wide range of other innovative contemporary poets (including Rothenberg, John Cage, Charles Bernstein, Ron Silliman, Lyn Hejinian, and Susan Howe), the modern is *not* over: the innovations and generative possibilities of artists such as Duchamp and Stein are not mastered, understood, assimilated, and, therefore, "over with." Perhaps one academicized version of the modern—mainly a limited narrative of high modernism and subsequent conservative retellings by T. S. Eliot and others—has reached completion, but as many recent critical writings demonstrate, one of the most exciting and invigorating tasks today is to reinvestigate the modern.[2] A rethinking of the modern has to do with a fundamental grasp of the possibilities for innovation put forward by a broad range of twentieth-century artists.

Rothenberg and Antin, in their complementary explorations of the primitive and the modern, are involved in an important political project. I find affirmation of my point in Sherman Paul's (1986) reflecting on the meanings of the primitive in the work of Antin, Rothenberg, and Gary Snyder. Paul claims that if any particular aspect of the primitive

> is focal, perhaps it is the political, for the good reason that these poets, dedicated to *poesis*, have entered the public realm and, to that extent, reclaimed the *polis*, the place of speech and act, that Plato tried to abolish. Plato also tried to banish the poets, and with this, the abolition of the *polis*, is a direct attack on the primitive, on the *muthologos*, as Olson says in *The Maximus Poems*, on the shaman, on the trickster. Politics, as we have come to know it, follows Plato in wishing to be rid of contradiction, opposing voices; and the poet, who by virtue of his vocation never loses connection with the primitive, is of necessity often at war with the state. (viii)

Precisely such a broadened *anthropological* orientation toward poetry—which is distinctly opposed to the more institutionally entrenched model of the personal lyric, or the mono-voiced personal narrative, each of which are taught on the basis of craft, repetition, and eventual mastery marked by "finding one's voice"—provides for a radically different answer to the question, What is poetry for? In opposition to mainstream academic poets who take pride in the "well-crafted" poem, Rothenberg (1981) rejects "the notion of poetry as elegance of expression" in favor of poetry as "newness of thought" (223). For reasons that are implicitly political and social,

Rothenberg (1981) puts forward poetic practices that may in fact be immodest and contradictory:

> Poets are not necessarily modest in what they set out to do, nor are mystics. I'm amused by this. I think it's absolutely wonderful and crazy that people should try to know the unknowable. (Not the unknown, by the way, which is a very different matter.) I think what happens is that you get a lot of contradictory propositions . . . and that helps to thwart the monoculture and single-minded total state. At the same time, my own approach is increasingly comic. (223)

In opposition to more commonly held (and taught) academic approaches to poetry, Rothenberg (1981) contends that

> Poetry has rarely been composed as an occasion for criticism (the "New Critical" poets may here be an exception). It has other, very different functions for those who make it, & may (as a process) appear in situations that aren't easy to define within the framework of "literature." When it does, all kinds of factors "outside" the poem—the intention of the poet, his relation to a community, the conditions of his life & time, his politics, the claims he makes to vision or experience, & so on—all these (& more) become important, even central. And the "criticism" that doesn't recognize them, that can't, with Cage, reverse the roles of life & art (& share that life, at least by way of challenge), can only obscure the function, push the poem into a different realm, one with far less at stake. (35)

Rather than an institutional model where literary practitioners take pride in juridical acts of judgment, valuation, and ranking, Rothenberg pulls apart the academic Fred-and-Ginger dance team—that is, the poetry-and-criticism team (remember Eliot's pronouncement that "criticism is as natural as breathing"!)—in order to enact poetry as a putting into being of a present-day living and thinking. In this sense, Rothenberg and Antin treat poetry with Emerson's expectation that holds the highest function of art to be *generative*.

Rothenberg (1981) advocates "a move away from the idea of 'masterpiece' to one of the transientness and self-obsolescence of the art-work" (168). Creation leads to further creation; reading inspires writing. And for Antin, Rothenberg, and Snyder, life should be lived in consonance with one's aesthetics. On the one hand, such poesis confirms the more explicitly political utopianism of Ron Silliman (1987) who claims that "among the several social functions of poetry is that of posing a model of unalienated work: it stands in relation to the rest of society both as utopian possibility and constant reminder of just how bad things are" (61). On the other hand such poesis affirms the inextricable relationship found in the story about John Cage's response to an annoyed listener to Cage's composition without musical notes, *4'33"*. The listener says, with considerable impatience verging on anger, "I could do that." Cage responds, "but you won't." And the reason the listener won't is that composition, as Cage, Antin, Rothenberg and others show us, is inseparable from living and from the governing models of consciousness that determine who teaches what in which venue and how "creative" writing differs from "criticism."

Even in an age that tends to discount the relevance and impact of poetry, the poetic practices of Antin (particularly in his talk-poems of the last twenty years) and Rothenberg (perhaps most dramatically in his "total translations," his readings, and his anthologies) inhabit a charged and important cultural site. As Cary Nelson (1989) reminds us, "poetry is the literary genre that is most consistently, thoroughly, and unreflectively idealized" and "literary idealization is thus necessarily in dialogue with, and embedded in, all the other idealizations by which our culture sustains and justifies itself" (245–46, 130). In one of the most insightful statements articulated recently, Nelson warns us that

> In the competition to define and dominate our sense of what poetry is and can be, quite different notions of what poetry can do within the culture are validated and rejected. In the dominant mode of literary history, such issues are suppressed in favor of a narrowly aesthetic history of the conflicts between different kinds of poetry. We need to recognize that poetry throughout the twentieth century is the site of a much broader cultural struggle. It is a struggle over whether poetry can be an effective and distinctive site for cultural critique, over whether poetry will offer readers subject positions that are reflective and self-critical, over whether poetry can be a force for social change, over what discourses poetry can plausibly integrate or juxtapose, over what groups of readers will be considered valid audiences for poetry, over what role poetry and interpretation of poetry can play in stabilizing or destabilizing the dominant values and existing power relations in the culture as a whole. (245)

Rothenberg and Antin destabilize dominant cultural values, and they do so in part through the disruptive powers of song and speech. For

Rothenberg, as in "Old Man Beaver's Blessing Song," or in his "total translations" of the Navajo Horse Songs of Frank Mitchell (1970), the primacy of sound is the principal force for disrupting the ordinary business-at-hand that rules our lives. He enacts and prizes magic, spirit, and ecstasy, realms that practical Republicans teach us to ignore. And Antin's talk-poems enact thinking in a public domain. Instead of the sentimentalized intensification of poetic thinking as *recollection* or as a philosophy that shields itself from the grit of vernacular speech, Antin's talk-poems offer an instance of poesis as present-being.[3] Both Antin's talk-poems, made up on the spot and spoken in relation to a specific audience, and Rothenberg's sound-poems share in and extend a twentieth-century innovative tradition, that includes Stein, Duchamp, and Cage, artworks that have a disruptive, disconcerting immediacy.

In his essay, "A Poetics of the Sacred," Rothenberg affirms "the cry of the Dada poets of the 1920s to 'liberate the creative forces from the tutelage of the advocates of power'; and the earlier political-poetic assertion by William Blake that 'poetry fetter'd, fetters the human race'" (1995, 93).

Charles Bernstein (1992) contends that

> official verse culture of the last 25 years has engaged in militant (that is to say ungenerously uniformitarian) campaigns to "restrict the subversive, independent-of-things nature of the language" in the name of the common voice, clarity, sincerity, or the directness of the poem. (46)

Although formal innovation and eccentric language-enactments are often assailed as elitist or antidemocratic, in fact such criticisms mask a desire to impose a rather uniform version of self-representation:[4]

> Too often, the works selected to represent cultural diversity are those that accept the model of representation assumed by the dominant culture in the first place. "I see grandpa on the hill / next to the memories I can never recapture" is the base line against which other versions play: "I see my yiddishe mama on Hester street / next to the pushcarts I can no longer peddle" or "I see my grandmother on the hill / next to all the mothers whose lives can never be recaptured" or "I can't touch my Iron Father / who never canoed with me / on the prairies of my masculine epiphany." Works that challenge these models of representation run the risk of becoming more inaudible than ever within mainstream culture (Bernstein 1992, 6).

In a tremendously effective introduction to his talk-poem "talking at the boundaries," a piece that keeps returning to and considering the nature and effect of obstacles, David Antin (1976) says

> i had tried out the idea of the artist as
> obstacle   how perhaps instead of giving a more precise
> or glamorous form to the platitudes of the culture
>   the artist might propose himself as a sort of impedi-
> ment like sticking out a foot in a corridor and chang-
> ing the direction of the traffic.
>
> (52)

Antin (1976) is well aware that "the effect of an obstacle depends on its placement and direction of traffic" (52). Antin's talk-poems conflict with the ideal of the well-crafted lyric. In a (poetry) culture dominated by the ideals of the well-crafted lyric of personal epiphany and of the poetry reading as an occasion for recollection that erases process, Antin's talk-poems themselves provide a readily audible obstacle, even after twenty years of such activity.[5] And were we to look today for poetry's place as reinforcer of cultural platitudes, I would suggest magazines like the *New Yorker*, where even poetry declaring empathy for the hard lives of common people appears in a small box (on a page along with a sophisticated cartoon, some more centrally prominent prose writing, and advertisements for furs, jewelry, fine foods, and exotic vacation spots). In such a context, the poem in no way disrupts the surrounding and predominating cultural advertising metier. Indeed, the poet and the poem submit to and reinforce the cultural priorities reflected in the layout of the page.

Sherman Paul (1986) observes that the cultural position of Antin and Rothenberg is akin to that of the shaman, whose role of vision and healing inspires Rothenberg's version of the poet to take "on the necessary work of *turning the mind upside down*" (99). For Antin, the thinking enacted in his talk-poems bears a strong resemblance to William Doty's (1986) description of a critical engaged version of mythography:

> Mythography, critically pursued, may function as a curettage device, scalpeling away debris (from our present perspective) that should have been removed long ago. But it also may provide us with some of the tools for making moral choices among the vast range of myths that are available to us; it should provide us with a heightened dedication to

forge the best possible personal and cultural mythostories, the stories that can serve as symbolic constructions of reality leading to individual freedom and social growth rather than a retreat into an automatically repeated and uncritical view of historical events that now may need to be drastically reshaped (19).[6]

Rothenberg's "A Personal Manifesto" (1966) begins with the declaration "I will change your mind" and that manifesto ends with a provocative recasting of Jesus: " '& if thou wdst understand that wch is me, know this: all that I have sd I have uttered playfully—& I was by no means ashamed of it.' (J.C. to disciples, The Acts of St. John)" (in 1981, 51). Rothenberg's own reading/chantings confirm Doty's (1986) observation that "Myths provide opportunities' 'to perform the world,' that is, to engage in sacred play by reciting them or by ritually enacting them" (15). While Rothenberg's assertion of Christ's essential playfulness links Jesus to a long line of (sacred) tricksters, such a characterization (along with Doty's phrase "sacred play") places the poetic activities of both Antin and Rothenberg squarely within the anthropological framework posited by Victor Turner (1982), who regards liminal situations "as the settings in which new models, symbols, paradigms, etc., arise—as the seedbeds of cultural creativity" (28).

Antin's talk-poems present an irritation that is an occasion (both for Antin and for members of the audience) for questioning and/as thinking:

> because the one who comes there and has
> been thinking of talking is a kind of agent provocateur   he is
> the one who comes bringing the troubles and has been preparing
> to unpack his pandoras box of them and leave them with you
> for your entertainment
>
> (1984, 220)

Antin's performance is fundamentally pedagogical, though not especially didactic. Rather, it is a process of withdrawing certainties. In its often rambling form, with starts and stops, misdirections, cul-de-sacs and avenues, there is a Thoreauvian productive idling at work (and at play) in an Antin talk-poem. First-time listeners often wonder about the *point* of his rambling stories and conjectures. Such a reaction might be juxtaposed with Turner's (1982) observation: "Dumazdier thinks that it is significant that the Greek word for having nothing to do (*schole*) also meant 'school' " (36).

Antin's form of talk is intentionally "sacred play," provocation, and unprofessional conduct:

he had not

had a good career and he wound up on a crucifix   and it is not
the aim of the ministry to wind up on a crucifix   its not
professional   there is no profession in being crucified
because one of the things about being a professional is you
assume there is a body of doctrine that can be taught and learned
that you can have a tradition   and it is not good to have a
tradition that puts itself to an end you dont hope to educate
people to do this and say the first step is here   this is the next
and then you can look forward finally to that   which is your
end   they dont intend to teach that in the church as a
profession   because thats intended to create chaos   which
no profession   wants and the intention of jesus was to provoke
chaos it was not to produce peace on earth and the continuity of
life   jesus said i bring not peace but a sword   and he meant
it   he got himself crucified in order to cause a great deal of
trouble   it was supposed to put an end to an untenable world
as i remember   which is why he sent his apostles around
to say that "the end of the world is at hand"   and he meant
right away   im going to produce it by getting myself crucified
now as i said

thats not a professional position because a profession assumes
a world that you want to continue   and behave more or less
appropriately within

(1984, 227)

Antin's principal allegiance in such "unprofessional conduct" is to radical philosophical inquiry—a questioning and questing by means of language theory, by narratives, and by the presentation of unsettling and unresolvable situations.

On the other hand, Rothenberg's (1981) principal (though, as I shall suggest later, not absolute) identification is with the shaman:

> The act of the shaman—& his poetry—is like a public madness. It is like what the Senecas, in their great dream ceremony now obsolete, called "turning the mind upside down." It shows itself as a release of alternative possibilities. "What do they want?" the poet wonders of those who watch him in his role of innocent, sometimes reluctant performer. But what? To know that madness is possible & that the contradictions can be sustained (134).

Either route, the shamanic or the Socratic, unsettles "natural" or habitual modes of thinking. Each encourages and makes appealing subversion and questioning.

In that encouragement—in the commonality of that enterprise—there is a solidarity, a communitas, that complicates what I have rather monolithically been describing as the poet's function as *obstacle*. A communal vision of artistic activity involves a rejection of linear models of artistic genius and progress. Such a version of literary or artistic history posits a series of great accomplishments that are out of the reach of other artists and that serve as (proprietary) barriers. But the experience and writing of both Antin and Rothenberg contradict any such narration; each makes substantial and free use of previous artistic activity. Each of them experiences the work of predecessors as either irrelevant or generative, but not, as in Harold Bloom's model of manly contestation, a father figure's deed that unmans one until the father is overcome. It is a communal version of the avant-garde which Antin posits,

> and thats what
> i told this man in washington   or something to that effect
> and what i realized as i said it then   and realize as
> i say it now   there is something of an idea of the avant-
> garde in harold bloom   however inverted   and even
> he seems more at home with it than i am   a notion of first
> comers whose achievements were new and blocked the way to
> further achievements along the same path   an idea of
> patented inventions   each one acting as a roadblock
> and the tradition as a series of bitterly fought retreats till
> the last "strong" poet finds himself like kafkas rodent
> or a beckett character backed into the last corner of the
> room   it is a funny view of a tradition having it back
> you into a corner   and comically a little like clement
> greenbergs versions of modernist painting   in which the
> brilliant achievement of one artist closes an avenue to
> the next
>
> (1985, 62)[7]

Likewise, Rothenberg (1981) has little use for a conceptualizing of the avant-garde that relies on closure and unapproachability. His own participation in the avant-garde defies linear models in favor of the making of breadth and open-ended opportunities: "If there's still any sense in talking of an avant-garde, then that must be it for me: an insistence that the work deny itself the last word, because the consequences of closure & closed mind have been & continue to be horrendous in the world we know. . . . [W]e must no longer think in terms of a single 'great tradition' but can open to the possibility of getting at the widest range of human experience" (4). Rather than poesis as an attempt to put a form of artistic activity out of the reach of other artists, Antin's version of accomplishment is, like Rothenberg's critique of "masterpiece" art, contingent and social, directed in part at other artists who might be able to make use of it:

> and i did the best i could   under the
> circumstances   of being there   then   which is my
>   image of what an artist does and is   somebody who does
> the best he can   under the circumstances   not about
>   making it new or shocking   because the best you can do
> depends upon what you have to do and where   and if you have
>   to invent something new to do the work at hand you will   but
>   not if you have a ready-made that will work and is close at
> hand and you want to get on with the rest of the business
>   then
>   youll pick up the thing thats there   a tool that somebody
> else has made   that will work   and youll lean on it and
>   feel grateful   when its good to you for somebody
> elses work   and think of him as a friend who would borrow
> as freely from you if he thought of it or needed to   because
> there is a community of artists

                                                        (1972, 58)

Rothenberg (1981) suggests that "the function of poetry isn't to impose a single vision or consciousness but to liberate similar processes in others" (105)—an essentially communal, generative, and Emersonian definition of poetry. For Antin (1972) that shared activity also constitutes the basis by which an artist establishes his contemporaneity, "mainly because the truly contemporaneous artists of our time are known primarily to a community consisting of themselves. In a sense it is this capacity of the contemporary artist to recognize his contemporaries that is the essential feature of his contemporaneity" (99).

As I have found in my own twenty years of activity as a poet, Antin is exactly right: through work, effort, attentiveness, play and, more important, through generative affinities with fellow artists, one approaches the present. Residing in present artistic activity as an opportunity for renewal and innovation is not given to one by virtue of a birthdate. As earlier portions of my essay indicate, in my characterizations of mainstream poetry, the dominant stories do not offer an artist the chance to approach the present moment except in a narrowly professionalized sense.

For Antin, that issue of approaching the present, how to live in it and how to make art that is of it, guides the methodology of the talk-poem as he finds himself

> going to places   to improvise something   because as a poet i
>   was getting extremely tired of   what i considered an unnatural
>   language act   going into a closet   so to speak   sitting in
>   front of a typewriter   because   anything is possible in a closet
>   in front of a typewriter and nothing is necessary   a closet is no
>   place to address anybody   or anything   and its so unnatural
>   sitting in front of a typewriter   that you dont address any-
>   one   what you do is you sit at the typewriter and you bang out
>   the anticipated in front of the unanticipated
>
> (1976, 56)

Indeed, for Antin, the rejection of poetry composed in a closet comes from a recognition of a reading as an occasion that has the capacity to reinforce, rather than to negate, inherently social and interactive dimensions of enunciation.

Discomfort with the premises of standardized, "natural" poetry writing constitutes a principal affinity between Antin and Rothenberg. Ultimately, for each, a reinvestigation of the potentials and practices of an oral-based poetry unsettles habitual assumptions about both the value of writing and the nature of the book:

> the whole problem of our literate and literal culture has
>   been   to some extent   the problem of the totally dislocated
>   occasion   that is in this case the book   which goes out into a
>   distributional system unknown to us
>
> (1976, 56)

There are different possible solutions to this vexing problem of distribution, which is one aspect of the commodification of the work of art. Poets can confederate and take over much of the process of publication and distribution, as the Segue Foundation and similar organizations have demonstrated. And by virtue of their immediacy, Antin's talk-poems constitute an ingenious solution to potentially alienating distribution methods, in that Antin's talk-poems are simultaneously the creation of the works of art and their distribution and circulation.

In critiquing the "naturalness" of the book (as the best container of knowledge), both Rothenberg and Antin reassert and reinscribe the importance of an oral poetics. Antin, in the talk-poem "how long is the present," recounts some of his own ambivalences and his own gradual movement toward the form of the talk-poem:

> since i knew that i was coming to a bookfair i brought along a book
>   i dont know a lot about bookfairs and i didnt know much
> about what people do there   but i thought it might be
> appropriate to read here   i dont get invited to read anywhere
>   anymore   i get invited to talk because thats what i do
> talk   and this time i was extraordinarily tempted to produce
> a violation of my   form   and read a talk piece or part
>   of a talk piece   or moderately tempted   i was not
> sufficiently tempted but i brought a book   specifically this
> book   my book   so that i could have done it   read
> out of it   and i brought it not specifically because it was
>   my book and i was at a bookfair and wanted to advertise it
>   but mainly because i was curious to find out if i had any
>   temptation to read
>   and i dont   not at all   and the
>   reason i dont have any temptation to read or no sufficient
>   temptation has often been mistaken by others   that is
>   there is a kind of discourse   of which i am a part   about
> whether poetry is inherently oral   made in the mouth
>   or whether it takes its definitive shape in writing   and when
> i say poetry i mean poetry in the large sense   i hope nobody
> takes me for someone who composes quatrains while
> either speaking or writing   or even in lines because for years
>   i havent uttered anything that approached a line in any way
>   but i mean poetry in the large sense that sir walter raleighs
> history of the world is poetry or   kafkas castle is
> poetry   or any work that one can think of as a significant
>   attempt to take possession of the world   or some part of the

world   for experience through language
        but the reason
im not tempted to read is different i think than most people
suppose   the reason   my reason   is the sense that i
have in looking at a book   my book   not somebody
elses book   but in looking at my own book and feeling
            that as i look i lose my sense of the present   my sense
        of the present disintegrates for me as i read

                                                    (1984, 84)

For Antin, the movement toward and into an oral poetics, a poetry of talk, has to do with the fundamental issue of how best to inhabit the present. (I cannot help emphasizing the importance of Antin's rejection of the line as the fundamental unit of poetic construction; indeed, his poetry, and perhaps most of the innovative poetry of this century, may very well depend on the consideration of other units of construction—the page, a unit of performance-time, prose blocks—as fair game for poetry.) Antin's affirmation of orality is not without ambivalences. After all, in "how long is the present" Antin carries a book with him (his own book): he writes books, and he speaks to an audience at a bookfair. But in rejecting the "natural" assumption that at a poetry reading he should read from a book he has already composed, Antin offers and explores an alternative set of preferences (which, by contrast, may serve to expose our more habitual assumptions about appropriate behavior in such a context):[8]

                    i have a taste
        for the present   which i imagine you can forgive me
            if you dont forgive me im sorry   its a strong and peculiar
    taste   and the present is a difficult thing to have a taste
    for   its very difficult because   in satisfying it the question
        i always have to ask myself is   what is the present and
        how long is it?   how long is the present?
                    thats a question
    i take very seriously as a poet   i have a very strong commitment
        to the idea of the present   and at various times i have
        had different attitudes toward what i thought it was   and
            i thought if i came to a place   and had no words in my
    hand or mouth   but only my historical disposition to speak
        in a particular way   out of whatever particular background
        i had   that whatever i said and did would have to relate

                    to this place   and so in a sense i prepared to come
                  unprepared to this place

(1984, 84–85)

Such an activity, as Antin stresses, is not some deed of "purity" and "innocence" that somehow manages to evade contingency and historical deter-
minations. Quite the opposite: Antin acknowledges the particularity of
his development of the talk-poem. Such a development is historically and
personally governed. In Antin's case, perhaps such a form of *poesis* may
come out of his own Brooklyn–New York–Jewish–artistic cultural milieu,
of storytelling and a principally Jewish tradition of seriocomic standup
routines, or even out of a nineteenth-century American intellectual tradition of the lecture, as well as Antin's own activities as an art critic. Antin
acknowledges as well, in an earlier talk-poem, that his talking is also a
means of self-disclosure (though by means of, in Antin's case, relatively
impersonal acts of storytelling):

                    the only way
            that   i can conceive of myself   as a personality   is by
      an act   of memory   by an act of interrogation of my memory
          which is   also talking   the self   itself   is emergent
      in discourse

(1976, 10)

     Together with the translations, poems, and anthologies of Rothenberg,
Antin's talk-poems provide a crucial reconsideration of the value of orality
to poetry. Antin "hate[s] being the servant of a previous impulse" (1984,
148), a declaration with important formal consequences for his composition and presentation of poetry.[9] But Antin's oral-based investigation of
the present comes at a cost, which he openly acknowledges. What he does
in a talk-poem, given its improvisatory nature, may well, Antin states,
"violate my sense of good design":

                    this problem of the
            present tense   and this is very awkward   for me
        because   whatever im doing   i want to be doing it now
          at whatever cost   and there is always a cost

(1984, 150)

But that cost is not just one of shapeliness or design. In fact, Antin's
talk-poems tend to be very well-designed and carefully constructed, de-

Thinking Made in the Mouth   107

pending, as I hear them, upon a series of off-rhymed (or, roughly homeo-morphic) stories leading not toward resolution but toward a confrontation with an underlying question or conflict. What Antin "pays" in lost form, he gains back in restructuring and calling into question the nature of a poetry reading. Instead of the recitation of a prior act of poesis (modestly reinvigorated by a "live" reading), Antin's talk-poems expose and disclose his labors. Rather than erasing or making secondary a prior act of (written) composition in favor of making present a labor of recitation (as a poet does in a typical poetry reading), Antin's talk-poems allow a listener to witness much more of the poem's *making*.[10]

By contrast, the more standardized and university-accredited poetry reading features other priorities and values. If we examine the ritual of the poetry reading from some of the available ethnographic and anthropologi-cal perspectives, the oppositional nature of Antin's talk-poems becomes a bit clearer. If we assume, as in Victor Turner's mode of thinking, that a poetry reading is a ritual designed to affirm and to do certain things, several features are *irrelevant* to Antin's type of performance. Given the hegemonic value of the poetry reading, as an institutional prop for given ideologies and aesthetics, the poetry reading in its more "natural" (that is to say, customary) form reinforces a dominant version of the careerist poet as the maker of "well-crafted" lyrics of accessible, clear, personal expres-sion. It reinforces culturally approved models of sensitivity and creativity, and a sanctioned but limited realm of acceptable poetic rhetoric and dis-course. And it reinforces a notion of a unified subjectivity/voice.[11]

Antin, by contrast, gives a much greater emphasis to talking as a mode of exploratory, heuristic thinking and questioning; Rothenberg's readings take up the site of the poetry reading as a place to enact shamanic impulses by means of magical properties of sound. As Turner observes of similar cul-tural and ritualistic relationships to dominant institutions and values: "I see the 'liminoid' as an independent and critical source" (1982, 33). In this sense, the versions of orality put forward by Rothenberg and Antin inter-rupt business-as-usual, calling into question key elements of what we have come to recognize as a poet's professionalized behavior. These poets of a more oral emphasis function heuristically to disclose some of the simply-*assumed* aspects of being a professional (university-employed) poet today.

The oral poetics of Antin and Rothenberg go to the heart (and ety-mology) of myth: "*Myth/muthos.* Jane Harrison: 'A *mythos* to the Greek was primarily just a thing spoken, uttered by the *mouth*.' I take this from Olson, *The Special View of History*, where he reminds us that both *muthos and logos* mean 'what is said,' and that the poet, the *muthologos*, undertakes 'the practice of life as story'" (Paul 1986, 48). Such a poetics is not a rejection of the written in favor of a simplistic idealization of the oral, but a reemphasis and reinvestigation of the situation of orality within the professionalized domain of the "literary." Rothenberg (1981) responds

> to a conventional & deeply entrenched view of poetry that excludes or minimizes the oral; & I'm saying that the domain of poetry includes both oral & written forms, that poetry goes back to a pre-literate situation & would survive a post-literate situation, that human speech is a near-endless source of poetic forms, that there has *always* been more oral than written poetry, & that we can no longer pretend to a knowledge of poetry if we deny its oral dimension. (11) [12]

The range of such a broadened version of poetics is impressive: "I would say that I'm speaking of THE TRADITION WHICH TAKES VISION & CONFLICT AS THE ESSENTIAL CHARACTERISTICS OF POETRY; SEES THESE AS BOUND TO THE STRUCTURES OF THE POEM & THE DYNAMICS OF ACTUAL SPEECH; & TRACES A 'LINE' FROM THE INNOVATORS OF OUR OWN TIME & THE CENTURIES IMMEDIATELY PRECEDING, BACK BY WHATEVER ROUTES, TO REACH THE FIRST MYTHOLOGIZED SHAMANS OF THE LATER PALEOLITHIC CULTURES." (33)

Obviously such a broadened poetics has fundamental curricular implications that go far beyond current anthology and canon debates. The inclusiveness of Rothenberg's poetics—as his many anthologies have demonstrated, particularly *Technicians of the Sacred* (1985) and *America a Prophecy: A New Reading of American Poetry from Pre-Columbian Times to the Present* (Quasha and Rothenberg 1974)—make even the more praiseworthy of recently reconceived American Literature anthologies such as the celebrated Heath collections seem tame, narrow, and inadequate.

The cooperative working relationship between Antin and Rothenberg is such that their poetic projects have reciprocal effects, invigorating our sense of the modern as well as the primitive. The interaction and reinvestigation of the two poetries, principally by means of a renewed attention to the possibilities of speech and song, leads to fundamental redefinitions of poetry and of poet:

> the range of the tribal poets was even more impressive if one avoided a close, European definition of "poem" & worked empirically or by analogy to contemporary, limit-smashing experiments (as with concrete

poetry, sound poetry, intermedia, happenings, etc.). Since tribal poetry was almost always of a larger situation (i.e., was truly intermedia), there was no more reason to present the words or the pictographs arising from the same source. Where possible, in fact, one might present or translate all elements connected with the total "poem." (Rothenberg 1981, 96)

Such re-search, by means of comparison and translation, leaves us open to consider that therefore "the modern poem is open to everything; that it becomes the vehicle for 'anything the mind can think'" (106). Of equal fundamental importance, such a view of poem and poet implies a self-resistant means of anticommodification and a healthy antiprofessionalism: "With such means at his disposal, the poet can enter on a career as a prophet & revolutionary, a cultist or a populist by turns. Or he can, in a more profound sense, become the person who keeps raising alternative propositions, eluding the trap of his own vision as he goes" (106). Rather than advocating the currently entrenched institutional model of the poet—where the developing writer is encouraged to "find his voice," to make a series of poems that show some range but a consistent and recognizable (professional) identity—Rothenberg and Antin point toward a career of poesis as a process of thinking and investigating possibilities, a process that is intentionally self-evading. The contemporary institutional model of craft-training rests upon the commercial visual arts model: an artist succeeds in commodifying his or her work by creating a recognizable (and thus privatized and commodified) style. That is, the commodified work of art has a certain signature to it that marks it as salable private property. But Antin and Rothenberg urge a career in poetry where such self-imitation is one of the traps to be avoided.

In a shared resistance to some forms of poetry's commodification, Antin and Rothenberg each (differently) present an interesting critique of writing and the book. Antin (1976) argues that

> writing is a form of fossilized talking   which gets put
> inside of a can   called a book   and i respect that can   its a
> means of preservation   or maybe we should say in a frozen food
> container called a book   but on the other hand if you dont know
> how to handle that frozen food container that icy block will never
> turn back into talking   and if it will never turn back into talking
> it well never be of any use to you again

$$(45-46)^{13}$$

Similarly, Rothenberg (1981) suggests, "writing, that strange aid to memory, eventually becomes its surrogate, displaces memory itself—the first, great Muse" (131). Rothenberg notes that this displacement "follows roughly the stages (torah, mishna, kabbal, magic & folklore, etc.) by which the 'oral tradition' ('torah of the mouth') was narrowed and superseded by the written" (121).

Their critique of the written, as in Antin's (1976) remaking of the site and activity of the poetry reading, depends upon a preference for process over product:

> its harder to understand what an oral culture is doing when its
>   making art   say   and easy enough to understand about stories
>   and talking   but you want to know what about pots?
>   because pot making is one of the things they do in oral cultures
>   some of them   and some people call those pots art   if
>   this pot making is art   its the art of making pots   its not the
> pots that are the art   pots are the outcome of the art
>
> (192)

Antin (1976) makes such an assertion precisely because, as he notes, it is far too easy to "convert the act of meaning into the object of meaning" (202). Thus Antin (1984) emphasizes process over product,[14] and proposes a distinction between making and distributing poetry:

> when
>   i went somewhere i wanted to make things happen   because
> it seemed to me that the art of poetry was the act of making
>   poetry not distributing it   and the act of going around reading
> from a book id already written seemed to be the act of a publisher
>   more than a poet   though it may be basically useful to us as
>   poets   and there is a sense in which we all have to distribute
> our lives to make them effective
>
> (151)

Antin acknowledges the necessity and desirability of the work's distribution—indeed his talk-poems merge the activity of making and distributing.

While speech itself is Antin's medium, he is not naive about its limitations. Books as such have many of the limitations that Antin and Rothenberg (each the author of many books) point out; but then

everything has its problem   talking also
        has its inherent difficulties   there is no such thing as a
    perfect medium   thats why they call it a medium   because
its in the middle   so to speak   its between   it mediates

> (Antin 1984, 56)

In his transcription of a talk-poem, Antin (1984) transforms a speech-event by placing it in another medium. He transcribes it

            in the hope of finding what in it was the real thing
        the real action   and i try to get it into the book in such a
    way that its still intelligible when it goes into this rectangular
        object with covers that you open   like this   and which
    is partitioned arbitrarily by those things they call pages
                there are
    no pages when i talk   you dont turn anything at   all that
        is   i turn you turn but we dont turn pages

> (56)

Such a play on "turning" plays off of poetry's misidentification with verse, which literally means a turning. Antin's talk-poems do focus on turning; they offer a listener an occasion to turn his or her thinking in other directions.

Antin's talk-poems, then, place him in a kind of existential crisis, but one that he approaches with humor and with the resources of an improvisatory vernacular. Admittedly, Antin's is a broad vernacular, including the discourses of linguistics, philosophy, Yiddish, anthropology, poetry, art, art criticism, and so forth. Antin's talk-poems put him on the spot; each one—and this is the tension built into such a performance—holds him accountable before an audience, accountable to make something then and there, and to answer certain fundamental questions:

    we come back again to   "what am i doing here?"
    what is it that im doing here?   im trying to find out   how i
    could find out   and what im trying to find out is by
        essentially doing what i think talking does   that is
        talking and thinking may not be the same thing   but i see
    thinking as talking   i see it as talking   to a question   which
    may give rise to another question

> (1976, 20)

Of course, that is what professionalized activity *never* does: put itself into question. A "regular" poetry reading does not overtly call into question the value of honoring a previous impulse and a preestablished script. In a sense, Antin's version of the poet bears a strong relationship to the work of the ironist as put forward by Kierkegaard in *The Concept of Irony*, where master ironists such as Socrates and Christ are marked by their ability to challenge fundamental assumptions by questions that gradually withdraw the content from no-longer-tenable assumptions.

In his introduction to the first talk-poem in *Talking at the Boundaries*, Antin (1976) makes a similarly audacious suggestion, one that flies in the face of "correct" professional behavior for a poet:

> i had suggested that i had always had mixed feelings
> about being considered a poet   "if robert lowell is a
> poet i dont want to be a poet   if robert frost was a
> poet i dont want to be a poet   if socrates was a poet
> ill consider it"
>
> (1)

For Antin, then, there is a close identification among talking, thinking, and questioning. Such linkages help to explain his rather complex and unusual theory of narrative, a theory that emphasizes questions, problems, and knots. An investigation of narrative lies at the heart of Antin's considerations of what it means to be a poet. Narrative involves processes of remembering, and often Antin's talk-poems both present narratives and reflect upon the nature of such narratives. Antin's presentation of narrative is distinctly social as the narratives and other elements of a talk-poem become a medium through which Antin and an audience become attuned to one another:

> now the point of doing these pieces
> for me   is that it gives me a chance   by a kind of subtle but
> ordinary human concentration   to get a sense of where youre
> coming from and how   and to allow that sense to put some
> pressure on my own way of moving
>
> (1984, 167)

Antin's knowing emphasizes movement: "my knowing which is really a way of going not of standing" (168). As a social interaction, his public thinking relies on processes of tuning (which is the title for a collection of his talk-poems [Antin 1984]). Such tunings, or attunings, involve resistances between listener and speaker, as well as internal resistances within Antin's own presentation and consideration of unresolvable narratives. Antin counts on these internalized responses as part of what energizes his public process of thinking aloud. Our relationship to an Antin talk-poem thus enacts metaphorically a whole range of other tunings, such as our relationship to one another, to works of art, and to the ecosystem we live in.

Antin's talk-poems put us (and him) in a place that poses a problem. One of Antin's terms for such a place is a dialogue, as in the talk-poem "dialogue" where he asserts, for example, that "the collision of the idea of christ and the idea of jesus was the dialogue of christianity   its basic problem framed as a dialogue   and a severe one   between a man called jesus and a god called the christ" (224). At the center of such dialogue is a paradox or a conceptual knot: " 'a crucified god'   it fits all right in your mouth but you cant quite think it" (1984, 224). In narrating the difficulties of a Lutheran friend who questions his calling to the ministry, Antin points toward his own concern with a particular version of narrative. Antin's friend, who contemplates the jesus/christ paradox, is troubled in part because for such a problem "he couldnt extract its root" and he ends up "despising and loving himself   despising himself for his doubt and loving himself for his doubt and for despising himself for his doubt" (224). Antin's talk-poems are extended instances of what fits "in your mouth" but what can not be thought through to conclusion.

Antin's narratives, as in "The Price," delivered in 1986,[15] point toward unresolvable questions. Antin begins "The Price" by proposing, seemingly casually, the principal conceptual nexus that will concern him:

> when i thought about doing this piece i intended to call it
> "where are you?"   because i wanted to think through some ideas i had
> about the self   and because thinking for me means asking questions to
> which at the start i dont have answers   this title took the form of a
> question addressed as much to myself as to you and was i suppose something
> of an answer or at least a response to a review of a talk i gave in new york the
> year before   in which someone complained that i suffered from a belief in
> the unitary self and had not enjoyed the benefit of french deconstruction
> which should have disabused me of this illusion
>   now even i have felt the french breath of deconstruction
> unimpressed with it as i am   but i am still interested in the self though i
> never thought i believed in its unity in so flatfooted a way as all that i always
> thought the idea of the self was surrounded by questions and in fact what i was
> interested in were precisely those questions   and those were questions i spent

a lot of time asking because i didnt know the answers   for if i knew the
answers i wouldnt have any reason to ask the questions   and one of the
questions i'm interested in asking is what is the locus of the source or ground of
the self

(1989, 14)

Antin's talk-poems are both about his relationship to narrative and an enactment or present-being of that relationship. Antin's (1989) theory is that
"the self   however you may define it   is entirely constructed out of the
collision of the sense of identity with the issues of narrative" (15). For
Antin, it seems fairly evident "that the self could not exist without narrative" (15).

"The Price" represents Antin's most sustained attempt to explain his
theory of narrative:

now this may seem purely theoretical but i'm not interested in it in
a purely theoretical way   yet i would still like to distinguish in my own mind
what i mean by narrative
i dont mean story   everybody generally means story
when they say narrative   but i would like to distinguish between two things
one i would call narrative and the other story   and as i see it theyre
related but not the same   story is a configuration of events or parts of events
that shape some transformation   but narrative   or so it seems to me   is
a sort of psychic function   part of the human psychic economy and probably
a human universal   at least we identify it with being human   and it
involves a particular paradoxical confrontation

(15–16)

Antin's initial effort to describe narrative gets deferred in "The Price,"
though Antin is already identifying (in the overlap of story and narrative)
a crucial undercurrent of his most successful talk-poems: they offer us (as
well as Antin) an occasion or a place in which to undergo transformation.
For me, the experience (though not the rhetorical strategy) is like reading
the best writing of Thoreau; the reader/listener is called upon to question
deeply held assumptions about thinking, making, and valuing. Though
Thoreau is much more accusatory and bullying in tone, using sarcasm
much more than Antin, in each case we are confronted by an act of poesis
that calls us (in)to account.

As confrontation is essential to my experience of Antin's talk-poems, so
confrontation is essential to Antin's emerging definition of narrative:

now my sense is that the center of narrative is the confrontation of
experience   an experiencing subject with the possibility of transformation

Thinking Made in the Mouth   115

the threat of transformation or the promise of transformation   these two
possibilities adjust it a little differently   in terms of desire   and without

    desire there can be no narrative   but one of the fundamental things we
desire   is to continue to be

(1989, 16)

At the heart of narrative lies a double desire: "we want to be different but
we want to be us" (16). Though we seek transformation, which entails self-
difference (since we wish to become something other than what we are
prior to the transformation), "at bottom nobody wants to become something totally other" (16).[16] This knot of untenable self-opposition is the
energy source for Antin's narratives.

    Beneath narrative configurations that we experience as story, Antin
(1989) claims that "it is the engagement with the possibility of change that
is the fundamental issue" (18). The construction of a self occurs on a site—
analogous to the site of Antin's talk-poems, which exists at an intersection
of language, talking, thinking, and questioning—that is marked by various resistances, exclusions, and inclusions, "because every self holds itself
together   to the degree that it holds its self together   at a price" (19).
For Antin, "what narrative at its core celebrates or ritually reenacts is this
grounding of self" (18). This difficult choice of self-consolidation and/or
self-dissolution rhymes with similar choices for poesis, in which an artist
must choose between competing claims of consolidation/conformity (of
genre, career, profession, and acceptability of artistic activity) as opposed
to actions that resist, oppose, and interrogate preexisting choices. Though
Antin's own practices align much more thoroughly with the latter option,
he too is aware, for self and implicitly for poesis, that pure potential and
pure resistance, "this unlimited and indistinct consciousness is a delu-
sive and socially useless system" (18). Which may be why as interrogating
as his talk-poems are, Antin's talk-poems are also formally coherent and
carefully (if spontaneously) constructed. Narrative, as Antin describes it,
is that conflicting energy/desire that underlies the spewing forth of story.
The particularity of a given self and consciousness is formed, says Antin,
by the interaction of that consciousness with its troubling narratives:

    and ultimately it is a matter of whether that
consciousness perceives an impending event as a threatening transformation
    that determines whether or not we are dealing with narrative   so that a
particular consciousness chooses its narratives   though it may feel as though
    certain narratives choose you   but they choose you by the character of

your   consciousness to begin with   which is to say that by the grain of your
      consciousness your narratives are chosen   and by what they do to your
      consciousness your self is formed

(1989, 23)

At the end of an Antin talk-poem, we are offered not a moment of
closure (which is one of my chief criticisms of monologues like Garrison
Keillor's: they end with a manipulative moment of sentimentalized wonder, and thus they evaporate and have no ability to bring about transformation; they remain merely consoling forms of entertainment), but a final
story that ends in an enigma specific to the concerns that have energized
that particular meditative occasion. As with the story of Harry at the end
of "The Price," or the story of Antin's Uncle Irving at the end of "what it
means to be avant-garde," or the story of the Marine at the end of "talking at the boundaries," the conclusion to an Antin talk-poem plunges us
further into the complexities and irreconcilable demands of an issue that
has called for his thinking and ours. At their best, as in the end of "what
it means to be avant-garde," we are placed between competing demands
made on us by the emotional immediacy of a story and by a (rhyming)
conceptual engagement that arises from the talk-poem's framing conceptual issues: "and it seems to me that if you cant respond to that youre not
in the avant-garde" (1985, 71). We are left too with a sense of the price of
any accommodation that we choose.

Turning now to Rothenberg, I concede that entire essays and books
(for example, Paul 1986) might be devoted to his poetry, his activities as
magazine editor, and especially his many groundbreaking (and ground-
remaking) anthologies. I propose to investigate one facet of his contribution to an oral poetics: "total translation." In considering translation in
general, Rothenberg (1981) suggests: "To submit through translation is to
begin to accept the 'truths' of an other's language. At the same time it's
a way of growing wary of the lies in one's own, a point of vigilance that
translators & poets should be particularly keyed to" (93–94). Particularly
with Seneca and Navajo poetry, Rothenberg runs into the problem "that
we, as translators & poets, had been taking a rich oral poetry & translating
it to be read primarily for meaning, thus denuding it to say the least" (77).
Especially with the Navajo Horse Songs, Rothenberg has to decide

how to handle those elements that weren't translatable literally. As with
most Indian poetry, the voice carried many sounds that weren't, strictly
speaking, "words." These tended to disappear or be attenuated in trans-

Thinking Made in the Mouth 117

lation, as if they weren't really there. But they were there & were at least as important as the words themselves. In both Navajo and Seneca many songs consisted of nothing but those "meaningless" vocables (not free "scat" either but fixed sounds recurring from performance to performance). (77)

Rothenberg's solution, which he calls "total translation," is an immensely important activity that not only "opens up the canon" to Native American poetries, but involves a radical rethinking of the possible locations and natures of "meaning" in poetry: "Let me try, then, to respond to *all* the sounds I'm made aware of, to let that awareness touch off responses or events in the English. I don't want to set English words to Indian music, but to respond poem-for-poem in the attempt to work out a 'total' translation—not only of the words but of all sounds connected with the poem, including finally the music itself" (78).

By translating the sounds, and by giving the sounds of the poem a priority equal to that of thematized meaning, Rothenberg's total translations have the capacity to reshape our reading (and sounding) of poetry generally. Rather than evading those portions of the poem that cannot be recuperated in "meaningful" words, Rothenberg's sound-translations expand the realm of the "meaningful." As Charles Bernstein (1992) remarks in a slightly different context—Bernstein's more specific concern is with nonsemantic or extralexical writing—"the meaning is not absent or / deferred but self-embodied as the poem / in a way that is not transferable to another code or rhetoric" (18). In fact, it is Rothenberg's (1981) successful encounter with the nontransferable elements that marks his work in total translation as a major poetic accomplishment:

> It was the possibility of working with all that sound, finding my own way into it in English, that attracted me now—that & a quality in Mitchell's voice I found irresistible. It was, I think, that the music was so clearly within range of the language: it was song & it was poetry, & it seemed possible at least that the song issued from the poetry, was an extension of it or rose inevitably from the juncture of words & other vocal sounds. (86)

It is the overlapping space of poem, word, and song that resides in the meaningful-as-sound vocable of the Navajo Horse Songs that allows Rothenberg most fully to demonstrate the interconnectedness of so-called primitive (oral) poetries and twentieth-century experimental poetries (such as sound-poems, performance poetry, Russian Zaum poetry, Dada, and others) and thus to confirm "the primitivity of avant-garde practice" (Paul 1986, 132). In working out his method of total translation, Rothenberg (1981) decides to take a different strategy than David McAllester's literal transcription of the sounds in a Horse Song because "McAllester's more 'factual' approach—reproducing the vocables exactly—seemed wrong to me on one major count. In the Navajo the vocables give a very clear sense of continuity from the verbal material; i.e., the vowels in particular show a rhyming or assonantal relationship between the 'meaning-less' & meaningful segments" (87).

The result is a poetry that, in the case of the beginning of "The Tenth Horse Song of Frank Mitchell," looks like this in Rothenberg's (1968) total translation:

> Go to her my son N wnn & go to her my son N wnn N wnnn N nnnn N gahn
> Go to her my son N wnn & go to her my son N wnn N wnnn N nnnn N gahn
> Because I was thnboyngnng raised ing the dawn NwnnN go to her my son N
>   wnn   N wnn   N nnnn N gahn
> & leafing from thuhuhuh house the bluestone home N gahn N wnn N go to her my
>   son   N wnn N wnn N nnnn   N gahn
> & leafing from the (ruru) house the shining home NwnnnN go to her my son N wnn
>   N   wnn N nnnn N gahn
>
> (1968, 224); see also 1971 and 1972)

Rothenberg (1981), in recounting his process of translation, says, "I decided to translate the vocables, & from that point was already playing with the possibility of translating other elements in the songs not usually handled by translation. It also seemed important to get as far away as I could from *writing*" (87).[17] Rothenberg sees his total translation process as "contributing & then obliterating my own level of meaning, while in another sense it was as if I was recapitulating the history of the vocables themselves, at least according to one of the standard explanations that sees them as remnants of archaic words that have been emptied of meaning: a process I could still sense elsewhere in the Horse Songs" (89).

Particularly as his poems and translations call into question our customary homage to the (merely) written word, Rothenberg (1981) "would like to desanctify & demystify the written word, because I think the danger of frozen thought, of authoritarian thought, has been closely tied in with it" (10). Such a position is very close to David Antin's preference for doing talk-performances rather than readings and for the ragged layout of his printed talk-poems:

one of the reasons im talking rather than reading
is that i dont want to carry any more weight than talk   that is
this is as true or as important as it is and as it sounds   and
its no truer and its not any heavier   if i put in paragraphs it
wouldnt become truer or more important it would look truer

(1976, 80)

For both Rothenberg and Antin, such anti-essentialist thinking—
which resists the notion of timeless masterpieces, enduring monistic
truths, and authoritative/authoritarian modes of communication—marks
a peculiar and important relationship to spiritual and religious dimensions
of poetry. Of the two, Rothenberg is more commonly thought of as a poet
of the sacred and of shamanistic practices. As Sherman Paul (1986) asserts,

> What, after all, is the sacred? In a review of Eliade, Rothenberg says
> it is what we, the profane modern men and women of Eliade's ac-
> count, experience "through dreams and the unconscious"; it is a realm
> of "human experience" poets may again open for us. This has been the
> burden of his work as poet and pedagogue, and what has been remark-
> able about it is that he has avoided the "conflict between the culture of
> the interpreter and that of the creator" that Eliade resolved for himself
> by remaining primarily an interpreter. (122)

In the conclusion to his preface to *Technicians of the Sacred* (1985; the title
is taken from Mircea Eliade), Rothenberg characterizes his own endeav-
ors as an answer to "the question of how the concept & techniques of the
'sacred' can persist in the 'secular' world, not as nostalgia for the archaic
past but (as Snyder writes) 'a vehicle to ease us into the future'" (Rothenberg 1981, 189). However, Rothenberg's version of the sacred is no idealized
space of pure goodness and light, but quite the opposite. In a long letter
to Sherman Paul, Rothenberg clarifies the self-opposed nature of his relationship to the shamanic:

> Thereafter, on the down side of the book [*A Seneca Journal*] . . . I would
> point out the references to Indian failure & culpability (the killing of
> the beavers in "Alpha & Omega," the killing of the harmless snake by
> Richard Johnny John, etc.); the occasional irritation with pretensions to
> new "religions;" the change from Turtle Island to Snake Island (a more
> ambiguous renaming of America than Gary Snyder's); &, most impor-
> tantly, the refusal on my part to claim shamanship while keeping at
> some distance those who do, e.g. the prayer that ends "The Witness":

the old people will dream
ghosts will arise anew
in phantom cities
they will drive caravan across the land
bare chested   gods
of neither morning
shaman   serpent in thy final kingdom   leave
my house in peace.

(Paul 1986, 178–79)

In his "A Poetics of the Sacred," Rothenberg posits poetry "as a religion without assurances," and elaborates the paradoxical nature of such a religion: "the strange thing about it, for many of us, is that we so clearly recognize the origins of poetry in states of mind and in forms of behavior that we think of as religious in nature. And yet, speaking for myself at least and for many like me, our tendency has been to pull away from religion as such. It is a tension that I feel in whatever I've done as a poet" (1991, 2–3).

That tension, of a religion based very much on doubt, skepticism, and questioning—what Emily Dickinson called "that religion / That doubts as fervently as it believes" and described as "we both believe, and disbelieve a hundred times an Hour, which keeps Believing nimble"[18]—is most fully elaborated in the writings of Rothenberg and Antin that have to do with questions of their Jewish identity, an identity that, as one might expect, is based on refusal, questioning, and exile.[19] One way to think of such an identity (or faith) based on difference is to consider Charles Bernstein's (1992) interpretation of a remark by Kafka: "Franz Kafka once asked, 'What have I in common with the Jews, I don't know what I have in common with myself?' This can itself be understood as a Jewish attitude, but only if Jewishness is taken as multiplicitous and expressed indirectly" (7).[20]

Such a concept of self-opposition applies to Antin's version of the story of Abraham, Antin being drawn to "the way genesis poses abraham's sense of himself as jew against his fatherhood" (1989, 17), pitting these competing demands in a moment of choice. Though Rothenberg has edited a huge anthology called *A Big Jewish Book* (1978), he says, "in the end it isn't the idea of (so-called) 'Jewishness' that most concerns me—rather a specific set of language plays, feats of word magic & language—centeredness (in its most profound sense) that come to a visible point within the illusion of the ethnically specific" (1981, 143).[21]

For Rothenberg, the most important statement of his version of Jewishness occurs in his preface to *A Big Jewish Book*:

> —a sense of exile both as cosmic principle (exile of God from God, etc.) & as the Jewish fate, experienced as the alienation of group individual, so that the myth (gnostic or orthodox) is never only symbol but history, experience, as well;
> —from which there comes a distancing from nature & from God (infinite, ineffable), but countered in turn by a *poesis* older than the Jews, still based on namings, on an imaging of faces, bodies, powers, a working out of possibilities (but, principally, the female side of God-Shekinah—as Herself in exile) evaded by orthodoxy, now returning to astound us;
> —or, projected into language, a sense (in Jabès's phrase) of being "exiled in the word"—a conflict, as I read it, with a text, a web of letters, which can capture, can force the mind toward abstract pattern or, conversely, toward the framing, raising, of an endless, truly Jewish "book of questions";
> —&, finally, the Jews identified as mental rebels, who refuse consensus, thus become—even when bound to their own Law, or in the face of "holocaust," etc.—the model for the Great Refusal to the lie of Church & State.
> And it's from such a model—however obscured by intervening degradations from *poesis*, impulse to conform, etc.—that I would understand Marina Tsvetayeva's dictum that "all poets are Jews." (1981, 122–23)

Sherman Paul (1986) sees in Rothenberg's investigation of Jewishness an activity that most clearly focuses and presents a universalized human perspective to Rothenberg's work:

> Living in our time does not make it any easier to feel *placed*. For all of us. Because, as he knows, all of us, not only Jews, bear the burden of human history. Exile is not an experience or a theme peculiar to Jews—it is, for example, one of the things the Amer-indians and Jews of *Poland/1931*, those lost tribes, share. Rothenberg is fond of quoting Marina Tsvetayeva's remark, "All poets are Jews," because, as a non-Jewish poet, she learned that poets are not exempt from the kind of experience she associates with Jews. Yet such statements would have more truth if they were amended to apply to all of us. Because all of us—

isn't this the burden of Rothenberg's work?—have in his large view of human history been exiled from the tribe to the state, from the primitive to the civilized, and are still wandering in search of the primitive (Stanley Diamond names the project), in search of the communality that will allow us to be fully human. (126–27)

Though there is commonality (and perhaps even communality) in the experience of exile (and in the hope of communal recovery), Antin's (1990) exploration of Jewish identity, in "Writing and Exile," focuses on the overlapping concepts of exile and refusal:

> you know i'm a dedicated atheist   when i hear jews say god i dont
> know who theyre talking about   i should say "what theyre talking
> about"   when you say "who" its even more shocking   the idea that jews
> can address an omnipotent an omniscient figure   an all powerful all
> knowing being localized with intention   and do this with reverence
> strikes me as preposterous but also offensive   so my experience
> of that sort of judaism   raunchy old men with earlocks who drank too
> much and read from books of prayer that when translated into english
>   became more offensive than they sounded when you only had a vague
>   notion of what they meant   this was my experience   from a few
> distant elderly relatives   and there were not too many of them
>   my family
> comes from a kind of left wing of the jewish tradition   the haskalah
> background   my grandfather was a hebrew scholar turned spinozan   and
>   there was a family of marxists   chessplayers hustlers   the part
>   of the family i liked   so to me jewishness was the sense of
> refusal   all these refusals
>
>   (1990, 50)

Antin's Jewishness-as-refusal is a cornerstone of the cultural poetics I have been tracing in this essay. It is essential to the skeptical, questioning thinking I have identified with Rothenberg and Antin. In "Writing and Exile," Antin (1990) says "my sense of exile was then beginning with an examination of what i was exiled from   i was exiled from a kind of enthusiasm" (49). That exile is from virtually all forms of unreflected (and unreflective) enthusiasm—from poetry's dominant mode, from superficial philosophizing, from essentialist ethnic identifications, from "normative" expression, from writing as inherently superior to speech, from closure and conclusion instead of questioning, and from nationalistic patriotism. For Antin, it is a "kind of not understanding [that] was the beginning of my exile" (48). Crucially, such an exile includes a distance particularly from nationalistic enthusiasm, as seen in Antin's recollection of his dawning sense of distance from American World War II patriotism:

> i remember there was a children's costume contest in coney island
> where the costumes were supposed to be based on a theme and the first
> prize went to a six year old in commando clothing with a blackened
>   face and twigs on his helmet with a rifle and bayonet called
> "dawn raid"
>   and this was a figure of a national allegory that
> celebrated innocent american violence   which was part of what i
> regard as the native experience   a construction of images for which
>   we have an unqualified enthusiasm because   they project a deeply
> satisfying sense of an "us" corresponding to a deeply threatening
> "them" whoever   they may happen to be   and in both of which we
> thoroughly believe
>
> (49)

In enacting (with Rothenberg) a peculiarly intense, comic, and compassionate doubting faith, Antin, in rethinking the story of his ancestor Wolf Kitzes's interaction with the Baal Shem Tov, speaks the oddly affirmative position of exile, a refusal that is at once artistic, political, and ethical:

> and taking pity on his great teacher he answered once again in the
>   jewish tradition   "so what should i have said" and left it at
> that   because there was nothing he should have said   because
> there is nothing you should say when youre addressed in this way   it
> is not an address fitting for an exiled human being at all   essentially
>   you must refuse this question because it is imbecilic   and my
> ancestor was distinguished by rejecting this degrading delusion even
> in the optimistic power of his love for the baal shem   because he
>   he must have realized that exile is inherently written into the humanness
> of the jewish tradition   which is the human tradition   and my
> ancestor must have known this and martin buber would probably have
> known this too if he had thought about it enough   if he had connected
> it with all those situations that buber had to have thought about in
> his reading of jewish history   in his immigration to israel   where
> jews have become a nation and there is no exile   only a national
> experience and a community that creates an exile for everybody who
> is not part of that national experience and happens to be there   like
>   the arabs   or the jews who are not part of that national experience
> because they havent yet learned how to hate the arabs and dont want to

behave like a nation which will behave like any nation
or writers who as writers cannot afford to be part of any nation

(52)

For Antin, and for Rothenberg, exile is a means of affirmation, providing a critical distance from faith-without-doubt, from a professionally sanctioned but noninnovative poesis, and from an enthusiastic but naively violent nationalism. Rothenberg (1981) concludes, "The only absolutes for poetry are diversity and change (and the freedom to pursue these); and the only purpose, over the long run, is to raise questions, to raise doubts, to put people into alternative, sometime uncomfortable situations, to raise questions but not necessarily answer them, or to jump ahead with other questions, to challenge the most widely held preconceptions in our culture" (223–24). As I have been arguing implicitly throughout this chapter, there is great cultural force and critical thinking in the poetic activities of Antin and Rothenberg. As Herbert Marcuse (1978) claims, "the critical function of art, its contribution to the struggle for liberation, resides in the aesthetic form" (8). And, as Marcuse explains, "it is not the business of art to portray the world as the possible object of domination" (36). The work of Antin and Rothenberg leads us into new and unsettling soundings and questionings; they do not offer us a mastered or masterable image of the world. It is that very lack of mastery, the contingency of thinking in the mouth, their *mythos*, that is generative of further thinking, singing, and making. Their cultural poetics and ongoing deed of *poesis* provide us with a pedagogy and critical presence.

> . . . it is so very much more exciting and satisfactory for everybody if one
> can have contemporaries, if all one's contemporaries could be one's
> contemporaries.
>
> —Gertrude Stein

7. Anthologies, Poetry, and Postmodernism

Several new anthologies provide an occasion to think through a number of thorny pedagogical and theoretical issues concerning postmodern American poetry. The three anthologies I examine in this chapter provoke a number of questions concerning the representation of postmodern American poetry.[1] First, is "postmodernism" a chronological term or an aesthetic term (or a mixture of both)? What is the relationship of postmodernism to modernism? A series of questions and choices revolve around the different functions and intents of anthologies, particularly the pedagogical implications of such collections: Do these books represent "the full range" of recent American poetry or (self-consciously) a specific segment of that output? What relationships are suggested between poetry and poetics, between the activities of poetry and criticism? To what extent do these anthologies allow poetry teachers to examine and teach the particular conflicts, arguments, and flashpoints in contemporary American poetry?

The three anthologies that I consider—Lauter (1994), Messerli (1994), and Hoover (1994)—are quite different in scope and organization. The Heath volume is a more general American Literature anthology, but it does include nearly 400 pages of poetry written after World War II. Here I make use of the Heath as representative of current attempts to define and put forward postmodern poetry within an increasingly multicultural framework of American Literature. Hoover's book—in keeping with the publishing traditions of Norton—looks like a traditional anthology: a substantial introduction that maps the various movements represented; concise critical-biographical introductions for each poet; a chronological arrangement by poet's birthdate; and a few selections by many poets: 411 poems by 103 poets in 701 pages. Messerli, whose anthology covers American poetry from 1960 to 1990, chooses to give more space to each poet: approximately 600 poems by 80 poets in 1135 pages. Though he does include a short introduction, Messerli's approach to anthology-making is to do away with nearly all explanatory frameworks, and thus he includes no headnotes for any of the poets nor footnotes for any of the poems.

Before considering the more focused anthologies of Hoover and Messerli, I examine Lauter (1994). I choose this particular anthology because the project of reconstructing American Literature taken on by the editor Paul Lauter has had a huge impact on all competing American Literature anthologies as they have responded to the seemingly groundbreaking multiculturalism and class diversity of the first Heath anthology (1990).[2] Within academic circles, the Heath has the reputation of being the most radical and innovative of the American Literature anthologies; in light of such an assessment, I focus attention specifically on Lauter's representation of modern and contemporary American poetries. The introduction to the section of the Heath called "Postmodernity and Difference: Promises and Threats" concludes

> Unfortunately for most readers, because women and ethnic writers have been less often anthologized, coming to know their work—and to understand its significance, especially if it deviates from what have become accepted patterns of literary representation—has been difficult. This anthology includes a number of comparatively young writers, many of whose books have been published only in the past decade. Our expectation is that the excitement to be found in new literatures expressing fresh themes and new understandings will be contagious to our readers. (Lauter 1994, 2822)

But that is precisely what is *not* present in the Heath poetry selections (nor in any of the "major" American Literature anthologies): deviation from accepted patterns of literary representation.[3] Oddly enough, the Heath does include a fair number of adventurous writings in prose and in drama, but in poetry—in which, perhaps except for the issue of multiculturalism, many American Literature professors seem to have lost interest—the range of representation does not constitute what might rightfully be called "diversity" or "difference." In *Canons and Contexts*, Paul Lauter (1991) explains much of the theoretical and practical groundwork for the Heath anthology. Lauter's project, Reconstructing American Literature, which led to the Heath anthology, is "designed to present and to validate *the full range* of the literatures of America" (1991, 37; my emphasis).

Like other writers about canon, marginalization, and representation, Lauter is aware of the competitive and snarly nature of making literary history (see, for example, Silliman 1990 and Golding 1984). As Lauter (1991) explains, once we have established a literary canon, it is "from this limited set of texts we project standards of aesthetic excellence as well as the intellectual constructs we call 'literary history.' And once we have developed such constructs, we view other works in these terms, whether the works originate from that initial text milieu or from outside it" (54). Lauter concludes that what is at issue (in the construction of a canon) is "survival," but he refers not to survival so much of "these works in themselves, but to the knowledge they make accessible and the experiences to which they give expression and shape—experiences which better enable new generations to comprehend themselves and their world" (59). In this sense—of works of literature as modes of consciousness and as modes of interpretive experience—Lauter's conception is, oddly, akin to Charles Bernstein's (1992, 17–18) definition of poetry as "epistemological inquiry." As Lauter (1991) concludes, for reasons of diversity and validation of different modes of consciousness, "we must begin by considering seriously the nature of the experiences we select for the classroom" (102).

But when we look at the Heath's (Lauter 1994) offerings in poetry, particularly postmodern poetry, we find a significant selection of multiculturalist poetry but an extraordinarily narrow range of modes of representation. This is not to say that all of the work is formally uninteresting. There are some exceptions from the mostly flat poetry of plainspoken personal experience: the bilingual poems by Victor Hernández Cruz and Tato Laviera, where the movement back and forth from Spanish to English foregrounds the conflicting contexts of the individual word; and a prose-poetry hybrid by Simon Ortiz, where "fact" and lyricism are placed in a productive crossfire. But for the most part, the poems that are put forward in Heath—as presenting difficulties, or as "the full range" of American poetry, or as deviating from accepted patterns of representation—are anything but innovative modes of representation. Lauter and the other Heath editors have simply substituted different subjects (meaning both speakers/voices and subject matter) for different modes of representation.

The Heath anthology provides a narrowly authorized version of the multicultural, one that smacks of an imitativeness of dominant white modes of representation. Many of the elect in Heath have been trained at conventional academic programs in Creative Writing, a large number at the University of California at Irvine or under the tutelage of one of the most conventional and highly awarded academic poets of our time, Philip Levine. Though the subject matter and subject position are different, the poems themselves are remarkably the same as their white counterparts in form, in voice, in diction, and in the manner of narrating experiences within the dominant mode of the personal narrative as crafted and developed over the past thirty-five years. An irony worth pondering is that under the rubric of diversity and difference, we are presented with poetry that extends the hegemony of a predominantly white, mainstream, highly professionalized and intensively regulated writing practice. Here are some passages that typify the multiculturalized version of the postmodern according to Heath:

> Last time I saw her, Grandmother
> had grown seamed as a Bedouin tent.
> She had claimed the right
> to sleep alone, to own
> her nights, to never bear
> the weight of sex again nor to accept
> its gift of comfort, for the luxury
> of stretching her bones.
> She'd carried eight children,
> three had sunk in her belly, *náufragos*
> she called them, shipwrecked babies
> drowned in her black waters.
> *Children are made in the night and*
> *steal your days*
> *for the rest of your life, amen.* She said this
> to each of her daughters in turn.
>   (from "Claims," Judith Ortiz Cofer,
>   2945)

> So, when it's bad now,
> when I can't remember what's lost
> and all I have for the world to take
> means nothing,
> I go out back of the greenhouse

at the far end of my land
where the grasses go wild
and the arroyos come up
with cat's claw and giant dahlias,
where the children of my neighbors
consult with wise heads
of sunflowers, huge against the sky,
where the rivers of weather
and the charred ghosts of old melodies
converge to flood my land
and sustain the one thicket
of memory that calls for me
to come and sit
among the tall canes
and shape full-throated songs
out of wind, out of bamboo,
out of a voice
that only whispers.
   (from "Something Whispered in the
   Shakuhachi," Garrett Hongo, 2967)
Above, in the rented rooms,
In the lives
I would never know again,
Footsteps circled
A bed, the radio said
What was already forgotten.
I imagined the sun
And how a worker
Home from the fields
Might glimpse at it
Through the window's true lens
And ask it not to come back.
And because I stood
In this place for hours,
I imagined I could climb
From this promise of old air
And enter a street
Stunned gray with evening

Where, if someone
Moved, I could turn,
And seeing through the years,
Call him brother, call him Molina.
    (from "The Cellar," Gary Soto,
3046–77)

Instead of the avowed poetry of difference, we get a deadening sameness of writing style under the auspices of the multicultural. Many of the Heath's "postmodern" poems — in the plain-style mode of the personal anecdote — begin like this one:

There was always something that needed fixing,
a car on the blink,
a jinxed washing machine,
a high-strung garbage disposal.
His life was one of continual repair.
            (Cathy Song, 3081)

It is, regardless of the ethnicity of the poet, the standardized American poem of the past twenty-five years: simple declarative syntax; the illusion of a craftless transparent language; a simple speechlike singular voice in the service of a poem that ends with a moment of epiphanic wonder and/or closure where all parts of the poem relate to a common theme. Clearly, there are alternatives. For example, among Chicano poets, why not include the genuinely challenging and difficult work of Alurista? Or among African-American poets, why not Nathaniel Mackey, Lorenzo Thomas, and Erica Hunt?

As contrast to the poems and passages I've quoted from the Heath, I present the following selections from Messerli's anthology as samples that depart from a single voice, personally expressive plain-style, anecdotal poetry:

superhighway elegy in a pink convertible / It was 1956 /
Sexy Propertius & his gal Cynth / Living Green Exotica /
Quaker Oats / First Chinese Dictionary (40,000 characters)
circa 1450 BC / Comes moon 1st fat, then skinny / seasons
skinny fat / as the world turns I blow my nose / Uniting
commonplace and cosmic / / Cosmi-comics: a woman in a tattersall
shirt is breaking & entering / "Poetry as breaking and

entering," he tossed over his left shoulder as he left /
over / Where were you all this time, damn you?

(from "Western Civ 4," Joan Retallack, 936)

an infinite statement. a finite statement. a statement of infancy. a fine line
state line. a finger of stalemate. a feeling a saint meant ointment.

tremble.

a region religion

reigns in. a returning. turning return the lovers. the retrospect of
relationships always returning. the burning of the urge. the surge forward
in animal being inside us. the catatosis van del reeba rebus suburbs of our
imagination. last church of the lurching word worked weird in our heads.

(from "Scraptures: 7th Sequence," bpNichol, 309)

Beside our bed a bowl of ready
   water, though we dance
upon the graves of the
   yet-to-be born.
          Awaiting
  birth,
     by which or in which a potter-god
could wet what clay would catch
   the flow of our endangered blood.
Here where the feuds root some
   unsunned angel of loss ekes out
    its plunder.
       Possessed,
we lick the salt of
    each infected wound's
   unyielding rhythm's wordings.
   "Whipped on, preached at, kicked.
Made a christ
       of.
    Whipped on, preached
  at, kicked. Made a
        christ of.
Whipped on, preached at,
   kicked. Made a christ
      of. . ."

(from "Song of the Andoumboulou"
Nathaniel Mackey, 1033–34)

To return, though, to the Heath anthology (Lauter 1994) aside from the problem of aesthetic xenophobia it exhibits toward experimental work, I am equally concerned with the model of the poet put forward. The Heath is genuinely excellent when it comes to representing the Harlem Renaissance. Writers such as Langston Hughes and Alain Locke are presented as thinkers and cultural critics of depth. In other words, we get selections of political poetry; of equal importance, we get intellectual prose. When Heath turns to the postmodern, the editors settle into the paradigm of the poet as intuitive artist. Where, for example, are the intellectually challenging essays by poets such as Audre Lorde (or Adrienne Rich or June Jordan)? Poets such as Amiri Baraka, whose poetry has gone through a number of difficult and transgressive stylistic forms, tend to get represented in simplistic ways. Both omissions result in a diminished sense of a poet's capabilities as an intellectual and as a cultural critic.

In the section called "New Communities, New Identities, New Energies" it is precisely the new energies that are missing. One does not dispute that Adrienne Rich's poetry is of immense significance. But what happens to the "other" *new* energies of feminist poetry? Where are Susan Howe, Rachel Blau DuPlessis, Wanda Coleman, Erica Hunt, Beverly Dahlen, Kathleen Fraser, Lyn Hejinian, Leslie Scalapino, Joan Retallack, and so on? What happened to the entire realm of Language poetry? (Consider, for example, that Charles Bernstein has published twenty books of poetry, two major collections of criticism, received a Guggenheim, and is translated and read in more than twenty other countries. His work is not in the Heath nor in *any* of the "major" American Literature anthologies.) What happened to the writings of "senior" innovative poets such as David Antin, Jerome Rothenberg, and John Cage? My quarrel is with the narrow range of "new energies" and "new representations" that are allowed between the covers of the "new" American Literature.

Unlike the Heath, Douglas Messerli's *From the Other Side of the Century: A New American Poetry, 1960–1990* (1994) does not claim to represent all American Literature (nor even all of of recent American poetry). It is an anthology devoted to the range of recent innovative poetries; as such it is both a treasure and a confusion. Messerli is aware of some of the difficulties and liabilities of the entire enterprise of anthology-making. He acknowledges explicitly the ghost or heroic model behind the current wave of anthologies of new poetry (including his own): Donald Allen's 1960 *New American Poetry*. Messerli contends that "we" need a new anthology that would have a similar excitement and impact as the Allen anthology. He critiques other anthologies as being either too limited in the selections made from poets' work (and that is, in my opinion, a problem with Hoover's (1994) *Postmodern American Poetry*) or as falling prey to an editor's overpersonal agenda. Messerli acknowledges that all anthologies are personal, though he claims that his goal has been to represent a *range* of aesthetic choices. To his credit, he has done so.

The poetry in Messerli's book begins oddly and provocatively with work by Charles Reznikoff, whose marvelously flat, realistic story-poems point, by implication, to the many varieties of poetry to be represented in Messerli's anthology. While Reznikoff's use of paste-up methods (as in *Testimony*) does link his work with modernist and postmodernist collage practice, placing his work first is but one example of the thought-provoking richness of Messerli's book. Unlike the Norton/Hoover tendency to give the reader predigested, carefully introduced examples, Messerli's book—which does not include any notes or introductions—can and will provoke thinking (in ways that are excitingly unpredictable). The range and richness of writings in Messerli's book will offer both confusions and surprises to any reader no matter how well read he or she may be. Whereas Norton/Hoover errs on the side of overauthoritative framing remarks, Messerli—who presents only an enigmatic brief introduction and a concluding list of publications by the poets—fails to provide a helpful (or pedagogically considerate) context for the poetry in his anthology.

In his introduction, Messerli discusses some elements of his anthology-making. He consciously chooses to avoid certain well-known poems, thus turning his anthology away from a "golden oldies" or "greatest hits" format. But for teaching purposes, certain touchstone poems *ought* to be there, otherwise the anthology becomes a book principally for readers already familiar with the touchstone poems of the era. I think, for example, of poems such as Oppen's "Of Being Numerous" (1968), Duncan's "Often I Am Permitted to Return to a Meadow" (1960), Ashbery's "Self-Portrait in a Convex Mirror" (1975), and John Cage's mesostics and chance-generated poems, all of which merit representation in Messerli's anthology and all of which are omitted.

Each anthology, implicitly or explicitly, serves particular functions. In Messerli's version of "a good anthology" the anthologist focuses on "poets who previously had not been extensively anthologized" and those poets who "extend and challenge the tradition of innovative American poetry which begins with Dickinson" (32). Considered in tandem, the Hoover and Messerli anthologies mark, among other changes in the volatile literary futures market, the continued ascendancy of Dickinson, Olson, Stein, and Cage, along with the decline of Williams, Eliot, and Stevens.

Messerli tries to give some sense of group accomplishments and relationships among poets (and thus he follows Allen's lead) in order "to illuminate some specific issues and concerns" (32). Messerli's anthology, while organized around individual accomplishments (and indexed and arrangement by individual poet), attempts to guide readers to issues, conflicts, concerns, and poetics. But Messerli's mode of grouping is coy. His book presents groups of poets—four of them—but he refuses to name them, but then he sort of does name them in spite of pointing out the fluidity of such groupings. He has one group concerned with cultural issues (including myth, politics, history, place, and religion); a second group focused on self, social group, urban and suburban landscape, and visual art; a third group revolving around language, reader, and writing communities; and a fourth gathered about performance, voice, genre, dialogue, and personae. Messerli's key guiding principle for the anthology is that "above all else, the poets in this volume are all extremely attentive to the ways in which language determines meaning and experience both for reader and author" (34). Messerli too acknowledges some of the limitations of his anthology: writers "whose writing has more to do with cultural, social, and political subjects than the more formally-conceived poems in this volume, must recognize the specific focus of this anthology" (34). But such a remark, which underscores Lauter's opposition of form and subject matter, presents a false opposition (between "politically concerned" poets and textually innovative poets). Such issues—particularly the issue of where and how a poem is political—are not best served by presenting half of an argument. An anthology might provoke more useful debate by presenting side by side poems that take opposite approaches to the political. The political dimensions of formally innovative poetry might best be understood in juxtaposition to formally conservative, somewhat didactic poems where the politics is manifest as "content" or theme or "message" or sentiment.

Messerli offers his book "as a travel guide" (34) not as a final destination. He provides helpful information about publishers and books by the various poets in the anthology, though a number of errors (such as having John Cage dying in 1933, for example) undercut the value of even this minimal informative framework. But, particularly with regard to pedagogy, there are some significant drawbacks to Messerli's mode of making an anthology. For example, by not having a selection of poetics—Hoover's anthology has a few, often short and quirky, samples of poetics—Messerli inadvertently truncates the range of poetic thinking provided and reinscribes a narrowed version of the genre of poetry and poetic thinking. Messerli also chooses not to provide the somewhat standard Norton-like critical/biographical introduction to individual poets nor does he make any attempt to provide a general introduction to the major movements of American poetry from 1960 to 1990. While these latter omissions may have an oddly beneficial pedagogy to them—that is, "if you're interested, go find out for yourself"—I do think that some guidance would be appropriate. If Messerli did not wish to write such an introduction himself, he could have pointed readers to excellent introductory books and essays by a range of critics and poets such as Marjorie Perloff, James Breslin, David Antin, and others. The end result is a massive volume—truly a great accomplishment—but one that offers little articulated context and almost no map or guide. As a collection of poems, the book is superb; as a pedagogical device, the book is lacking.

For the Norton *Postmodern American Poetry*, Hoover (1994), in a remark that points to precisely what is missing in Lauter's anthology, claims, "This anthology shows that avant-garde poetry endures in its resistance to mainstream ideology; it is the avant-garde that renews poetry as a whole through new, but initially shocking, artistic strategies" (xxv). Hoover's book keeps true to his aim of presenting postmodernism as many modes of writing: "This anthology does not view postmodernism as a single style with its departure in Pound's *Cantos* and its arrival in language poetry; postmodernism is, rather, an ongoing process of resistance to mainstream ideology" (xxvi). Even so, two complaints must be made: (1) How can a reader know what that mainstream ideology is without its representation in the anthology? (2) In spite of "our" rhetoric against "the" mainstream, is the mainstream in fact a singular practice or ideology (or is that not the rhetorical straw man of the [similarly multiple] avant-garde)?

In his detailed introduction, Hoover addresses some of the key conflicts, issues, and concerns within the plural practice of the avant-garde. He points out, for example, an allegiance to "a constructionist rather than an expressionist theory of composition" (xxvii), but he does not really delve into the ways in which a constructionist practice—that of Silliman or Andrews, for example—also carries with it important political dimensions (and thus Hoover can, at times, reinforce the formal versus political binary that Lauter and Messerli fall prey to). Hoover also points to an interesting split in the 1970s between poets (principally the Language poets) whose work challenged a speech-based poetry and poets whose work "extended spoken poetry into performance poetry" (xxvi). Such a split, as the recent poetry of Jack Foley demonstrates and as critical writing by Dana Gioia suggests, is at the heart of current debates over directions and new practices in poetry (see, for example Foley 1993 and Gioia 1993).

Most important, Hoover points toward a changing notion of meaning:

> As Robert Creeley has written, "Meaning is not importantly *referential*." Quoting Charles Olson, Creeley continues, "*That which exists through itself is what is called the meaning*." Thus the material of art is to be judged simply as material, not for its transcendent meaning or symbolism. In general, postmodern poetry opposes the centrist values of unity, significance, linearity, expressiveness, and a heightened, even heroic, portrayal of the bourgeois self and its concerns. (xxvii)

My chief complaint—and it is one I direct at my own criticism as well—is that we have repeated again and again such declarations of different assumptions and different writing practices but we have not yet been able to create credible or teachable new models of reading and criticism that take up such realizations of shifts in the nature of meaning-making. Most critical writing on the avant-garde still tends to be bound up in New Critical models of (theme-based) close reading. The attentiveness of close reading *is* appropriate to the reading of new poetries, but the habitual reversion to theme and/or subject matter (for the purposes of unification and a sense of mastery) is not.

Hoover proceeds openly and helpfully with his identification of important groups and movements in postmodern American poetry.[4] He describes contributions of the Beat Movement, the New York School, the second generation of the New York School, Projectivist/Black Mountain poetry, ethnopoetics (Rothenberg), the deep image, aleatory poetry, prose poetry, experimental feminist poetry, language poetry, and performance poetry. Hoover identifies John Ashbery as, since 1975, playing the leading role in American poetry. One could argue that an equally important position has been occupied by Adrienne Rich, who, interestingly, is not represented by either Hoover or Messerli. Hoover offers a provocative suggestion in putting forward Ashbery's preeminence: "Ashbery's poetry points toward a new mimesis with consciousness itself as a model" (xxxi). Perhaps a representation of consciousness, linked to a new realism *is* "our" central project. Indeed, many varieties of poetry claim to represent a contemporary consciousness, and these poetries, as the Hoover and Messerli anthologies demonstrate, go about the task in very different manners.

Hoover correctly notes the importance in postmodern poetry of collaborative writing projects. One might ask, Does such collaboration challenge the hegemony of individual authorship? More pertinent for this essay, Why is it that the anthologies do not represent collaborative poetry at all? Collaborative writing would fit in ideally with Lauter's perspectives on community-based cultural production and equally well with an avant-garde position of writing not as personal expression but as contructivist deed. The absence of such writing points to the powerfully conservative organizing function of the traditional anthology, which is decidedly based on individual accomplishment (even if those accomplishments, as in Hoover and Messerli, are contextualized by introductory remarks that point toward the individual's participation in broader group movements).

The case of John Cage provides another interesting litmus test for the anthologies and the representation of American poetry. It is gratifying to see his writing well represented in both the Messerli and Hoover anthologies. In fact, Hoover goes so far as to call aleatory poetry the "essence of postmodernism" (xxxiv). I can only note with disappointment and amusement the omission of Cage's writing from all the "major" anthologies of American Literature. While it would be hard to think of a poet more thoroughly American or political in his writing of poetry—I would be hard pressed to think of a case that better illustrates the intimate relationship between form and politics—the narrowness of Lauter's thinking about "the political" lands writing such as Cage's (which challenges the tidy definitions of genre and the bourgeois notion of heroic individual expression) outside the bounds of the acceptable.

One function of an anthology, particularly one devoted to the "new" in poetry, is to attempt (implicitly) an assessment of what innovations and directions are noteworthy and generative. Hoover argues that Language poetry and performance poetry "have become increasingly the dominant postmodern modes" (xxxv). Anthologies of the avant-garde inevitably confront the problem that David Antin noted in the early 1970s: the present is a difficult place to be or to describe; the present, particularly in poetry, is always open at one end. Hoover's principal goal, though, is to represent a "variety of experimental practice" (xxv). In this regard he does a good job. He seeks to counter the risk "that the avant-garde will become an institution with its own self protective rituals" (xxv). It is precisely this risk of wagon-circling self-enclosure that Messerli's anthology does not overcome.

In both anthologies—Hoover and Messerli—Language poetry assumes a central position in representing the vitality of experimentation in contemporary poetry. Hoover notes the way in which Language poetry necessitates a substantial involvement with—indeed a rereading and rethinking of—literary precursors. Language poets such as Charles Bernstein, Susan Howe, Lyn Hejinian, Barrett Watten, and Ron Silliman—along with literary critics such as Cary Nelson, Marjorie Perloff, Peter Quartermain, and Jerome McGann—offer a vigorous new reading of literary modernism, one that extends and pluralizes our understanding of what modernism was and is. Hoover points to Stein, Khlebnikov, Zukofsky, Olson, Mac Low, and Coolidge as important foundations for language poetry. Hoover concludes,

> Seeing a poem as an intellectual and sonic construction rather than a necessary expression of the human soul, language poetry raises technique to a position of privilege. Language poets see lyricism in poetry not as a means of expressing emotion but rather in its original context as the musical use of words. Rather than employ language as a transparent window onto experience, the language poet pays attention to the material nature of words. Because it is fragmentary and discontinuous, language poetry may appear at first to be automatic writing; however, it is often heavily reworked to achieve the proper relation of materials. This approach is consistent with William Carlos Williams's definition of a poem as a "small (or large) machine made of words. When I say there's nothing sentimental about a poem I mean there can be no part, as in any other machine, that is redundant." (xxxv–xxxvi)

As is inevitably the case, such generalizations oversimplify and homogenize a more complicated and conflicted literary practice. But Hoover's introductory remarks do point toward valid and engaging topics. For example, detailed investigation of the place of the "lyric" or "lyricism" in and of itself would make for interesting thinking about the postmodern.

Hoover, in one of his somewhat oversimplistic generalizations, claims that "language poetry, too, rejects the idea of poetry as an oral form; it is written" (xxxvii). It seems to me that this issue—poetry as speech versus poetry as writing—underlies both the Messerli and Hoover anthologies (and is why a writer/performer such as Jack Foley belongs in both anthologies). The ramifications of such an ostensible split, particularly as we move toward the end of the era of the book, will reverberate for some time. Oddly, even anthologies (as hardbound or paperbound books) of the avant-garde, as the book itself becomes reformatted by means of electronic modes of presentation, take on a conservative and nostalgic function.[5]

One troubling tendency of conceptualizations of the avant-garde has been its frequent manifestation as yet another domain of white male accomplishment. That is one reason, for example, that the overturning of a reductionist version of high literary modernism (Pound, Eliot, Stevens, Williams) in favor of a pluralized modernism that includes Langston Hughes and the range of accomplishment in the Harlem Renaissance (including Alain Locke's groundbreaking anthology, *The New Negro* [1925]), Gertrude Stein, H.D., and others, is significant. Messerli does not address directly the issue of ethnicity or multiculturalism in the making of his anthology. But his book includes a significant African-American presence, including important writing by Amiri Baraka, Lorenzo Thomas, Clarence Major, and Nathaniel Mackey. The presence of women poets, particularly in the range of writings covered by the term Language poetry, is significant. Textual feminism, including the work of Kathleen Fraser, Susan Howe, Joan Retallack, Lyn Hejinian, Leslie Scalapino, and Carla Harryman, is critical to an understanding of the significant innovative poetries of our time. These poets are well represented in the new Hoover and Messerli anthologies (but not in the Heath nor the other "major" American Literature anthologies).

Hoover concludes with remarks that have been implicit throughout the making of his anthology (and Messerli's too):

> The *fin de siècle* position of postmodern art suggests to some that it is in a state of exhaustion; in *Has Modernism Failed?*, art critic Suzi Gablik argues unpersuasively that "innovation no longer seems possible, or even desirable." In fact, the poetry now being produced is as strong as, and arguably stronger than, that produced by earlier vanguards. As history remains dynamic, so does the artistic concept of "the new." The period since 1950 will be seen as the time when the United States finally acquired its full share of cultural anxiety and world knowledge, and thereby its most daring poetry. (xxxix)

In different ways, the Lauter, Messerli, and Hoover anthologies make the case for the vitality and sweep of twentieth-century American poetry. But each begs the question of whether or not postmodern poetry differentiates itself (or whether or not it is even necessary that it differentiate itself) from modernism.

Many innovative poetries and Language poetry in particular make a claim to an altered relationship between reader and writer where the "reader [is] to participate actively in the creation of meaning" (Hoover 1994, xxxvi). Hoover explains that "a poem is not 'about' something, a paraphrasable narrative, symbolic nexus, or theme; rather, it is the actuality of words" (xxxvi). Such an oppositional truism pertains to most of the innovative poetries included under the heading of the postmodern. But such a truism, which has certainly been reiterated for twenty years or more, only begins to do the needed work of developing and demonstrating new reading/meaning paradigms that can be differentiated from the persistent New Critical paradigms. It is one thing to claim, via Stein, that innovative poetries return our attention to the word as such: "such a view disinvests the language of metaphysics and returns it to the physical realm of daily use" (xxxvii). But how do we articulate and write such a reading experience? Perhaps the Hoover and Messerli anthologies are launching points for the development of new reading and critical paradigms. At present, however, both anthologies are weakened (as pedagogical tools) by the lack of demonstration of how such new modes of reading and meaning-making might look.[6]

Why do we need and make anthologies in the first place? A principal claim is economic: individual books of poetry are expensive, and if universities are to teach contemporary poetry responsibly, an anthology is a financially feasible way to expose students to the range of choices available. (Of course, to use an anthology in a class does not preclude the use of individual books of poetry. I would guess that most professors do use both anthologies and individual books.) But all three anthologies — the Heath, Hoover, and Messerli — miss a great teaching opportunity: the chance to teach the conflicts. The key arguments, questions, and flashpoints exist by implication *outside* the covers of each of these books. For example, if I want to teach the vexed question of where we locate politics in poetry, I do not really have the fully conflicting examples in any one anthology. It would be nice, for example, to be able to teach Philip Levine, Carolyn Forche, June Jordan, Judy Grahn, Robert Bly, and Adrienne Rich on the one hand; and Ron Silliman, Erica Hunt, Bob Perelman, Bruce Andrews, James Sherry, and John Cage on the other hand. If the claim that poetry's politics is something that is subject- or theme-based (as in the more conventional, somewhat plainspoken examples of Levine, Forche, Jordan, Grahn, Bly and Rich) is to be challenged by another assumption (that poetry's politics comes as much from reader-writer relationships, from material choices of publication and distribution, and from the social relations that inhere in stylistic choices and embodiments), how much better and more instructive it would be to have the most fully conflicting modes of writing/thinking side by side in the same book. Or, to pick one other example, if the mainstream privileging of personal voice and personal expression (as in poems by Sharon Olds, Robert Lowell, and Gerald Stern) is to be challenged directly by a poetry of many voices and a poetry of sustained difference (as in poems by Susan Howe, Clark Coolidge, and Charles Bernstein), why not have an anthology with examples from both aesthetic domains? The widespread poetry of the personal, individual voice—the personal lyric—is virtually missing from Messerli's book and from Hoover's too. Such an omission denies the partisans of the avant-garde the opportunity to find out that poetry of the personal voice has its own elements of variety and self-interrogation, as in Rich's work. Such writing hardly exists in Hoover and Messerli, just as the more formally innovative poetries are banned in Heath (and every other general American Literature anthology).

I am suggesting that an anthology begin to represent (somewhat democratically?) precisely what Messerli advocates, a *range* of aesthetic choices, and what Lauter claims to present, "the full range of the literatures of America." As a pedagogical tool—which is one recurrent claim for anthologies—how better to get the job done? Without the examples that are truly in conflict with one another, anthologies reinforce the fragmentation of the poetry world and, wittingly or unwittingly, reinscribe the non-conversation at large. Though it is possible to teach the conflicts by using two or more anthologies, the lack of a single anthology that includes some key oppositions and a substantial conflicting aesthetic range is a deficiency reflective of segregated writing practices and conditions within and without academia. I am *not* arguing that, with a little tinkering, one anthology could or would cover everything of significance in contemporary American poetry. Anthologies will inevitably (and, at times, constructively) be partial. But I believe that one way to restore poetry to a position of importance in the contemporary curriculum would be to make an anthology that allowed for a heated teaching of the conflicts present in contemporary poetry: the nature of a self, gender in poetry, politics in poetry, reader-writer relations, the conflicts between a written and an oral poetry, written text versus performance, manifestations of ethnicity and community in poetry, the rhetorics of lyricism and sincerity, and thematic versus textual feminism.

We also should give some thought to the timing of these anthologies. Are they not perhaps among the last such books, anthologies appearing at the end of a book culture? As Heath and others move into on-line discussion groups and computer-generated syllabi and supplements, shouldn't books of innovative poetry be looking toward new organizations of printed matter? Messerli's anthology is outstanding in its representation of different visual/oral texts (see, for example, the work by Darragh, Templeton, Weiner, Retallack, Cage, and McCaffery). But won't the anthology, as it is digitalized, become a more malleable entity, subject to reorganization by students/readers/users? No doubt, the next wave of poetry anthologies, poetry that is post-postmodern, will mark a departure from the fixed medium of a bound book culture.[7]

Conclusion

At the end of *Issues and Institutions*, the first of two volumes for *Opposing Poetries*, I offer not overarching conclusions but remarks made decidedly midway in a larger endeavor. The analysis of the politics of poetry's institutionalization that I present here functions best in conjunction with the more text-focused readings of Volume 2. At the end of *Readings*, I provide a more comprehensive conclusion to the entire project of *Opposing Poetries*.

Nevertheless, at this midway point, I shall indulge in some provisional concluding assessments regarding the current state of poetry's institutionalization. First, very recently, the study of that process of institutionalization has received perceptive, thorough attention. Two valuable books on the subject have just been published: Alan Golding's *From Outlaw to Classic: Canons in American Poetry* (1995) and Jed Rasula's *The American Poetry Wax Museum: Reality Effects, 1940–1990* (1995). Golding, whose book begins with "A History of American Poetry Anthologies," presents a historical account of the development of an American poetry canon. He begins with the first books of poems and first poetry anthologies published in America; thus his study offers perspective on the background for poetry's current conflicts. Golding argues for a position similar to my own in *Opposing Poetries*; he maintains that "'American poetry' has been from its beginnings a socially constructed and contested rather than a natural category" (10).

In order to understand better the dynamics of the current situation in poetry, both Golding and Rasula correctly turn our attention to the history and consequences of New Criticism. Specifically, each pays careful attention to the phenomenal success and impact of Cleanth Brooks and Robert Penn Warren's textbook, *Understanding Poetry: An Anthology for College Students* (first published in 1938; 2d ed., 1950; 3d ed., 1960). The history of New Criticism, particularly as it influences pedagogy and becomes a dominant methodology for the care, evaluation, and transmission of poetry within an academic setting, may be quite instructive for the current moment when a range of alternative and innovative poetries may have an opportunity to alter that institutional framework. Golding points toward New Criticism's basis in pedagogy and method. He notes that "between 1949 and 1976, total distribution of *Understanding Poetry* in its various forms and editions . . . ran to forty printings and 294,700 copies" (104). New Criticism, principally through *Understanding Poetry*, institutionalized methods of reading poetry and thus indirectly also shaped the process of evaluating and canonizing poetry. Golding cites Richard Ohmann's conclusion that New Criticism taught several generations of readers " 'how to write papers as students, how to write articles later on and what to say about a poem to our students in a 50-minute hour' " (108–9). And, as Golding points out, such methods—a theme-based reading of the poem as a unified text that achieves closure; the ability to restate the essence of the poem (typically, through a thematic assertion); the treatment of the poem as self-contained unit; and so forth—"extended beyond college classrooms to reach the secondary school student and teacher" (109).

It is this persistence of the institutionalization of New Criticism that Language poetry and other innovative poetries of the twentieth century must contend with and contest if these innovative poetries are to have a lasting effect within the better-funded (often academic) institutions of poetry. Golding and Rasula both link the New Criticism to the ossified institutional reading and writing practices that I discussed in Chapter 1. In fact, Rasula (1995) claims that "the New Criticism remains the most successful American literary movement of the century, though it's not generally recognized in quite those terms" (70). Rasula, I believe correctly, views that success in terms of the *institutionalization* of method:

> The dominant condition circumscribing American poetry in the second half of the twentieth century is its subsistence in administrative environments. From the New Criticism of the 1940s to the rise of the Associated Writing Programs in the 1970s, American poets could be sure

of one thing: regardless of whether they had access to a general public, there was at least the solace that certain bureaucratic precincts privileged poems as the raw material, the data, of administration. (68–69)

The New Criticism set in place what Rasula calls the "institutional custodianship" of poetry (76), not only by presenting a newly professionalized version of critical practice and by offering a detailed reading methodology through a textbook/anthology, but also by means of the proliferation of scholarly quarterlies, scholarly symposia, and summer institutes. In Rasula's analysis of institutional practice, "once their methods of close reading as applied to the lyric had gained approval, the New Critics no longer needed to control the poetic environment; it had become self-regulating in compliance with prevailing feedback principles" (84).

While the rise of degree programs in Creative Writing redrew the turf of the English department, the institutionalized reading methods (and thus also the principles of evaluation and support) were hardly disturbed. As I argue in Chapter 4, most current versions of multicultural poetry, while emphasizing some cultural and historical information outside the precincts of the autonomous New Critical poem, still leave unchallenged prevailing concepts of the lyric, personal expressiveness, the unified speaking voice, and the habit of (epiphanic) closure. In other words, even with the rise of Creative Writing and multiculturalism, the fundamental underpinnings of New Criticism's institutionalization have not been challenged.

And that is precisely one of the intriguing elements of Language poetry: it is one of the first fundamentally different poetries to challenge New Critical paradigms from *within* an institutional framework. In fact, one way that Golding approaches Language writing is to think of it "in terms of its possibilities for changing the mediating institutions from within" (146). While I shall focus here principally on the positioning of Language writing *within* an academic setting, it is equally important to recognize that for the past twenty years Language writers have operated with great energy and effectiveness *outside* of academic institutions. By means of independent presses and journals, reading series, newsletters, and alternative modes of distribution, Language writing has achieved a well-organized set of alternative institutions. But in the mid-1990s, we witness some elements of Language writing's residence *within* a more traditional academic institutional setting. Golding (1995) concedes,

It is true that in the current treatment of Language writing, we are seeing the canonization of an avant-garde in progress. This process mani-
fests itself in all the usual ways: an increasing number of critical articles
on and references to Language writing and individual writers; the presence of Language writing as a subject on conference programs, and the
poets' presence as speakers; books and book chapters, and dissertations
that have become or are becoming books; in a few cases, publication
with mainstream or academic presses. (147)

In a phrase borrowed from Rachel Blau DuPlessis's (1987) book of poems
Tabula Rosa (which I examine in detail in volume 2), Golding's chapter
on Language writing bears the title "Provisionally complicit with resistance." Haunted perhaps by Charles Olson's advice to Cid Corman and
others to resist the academic control of culture, many innovative poets
might assume that even Language writing's rather ambivalent relationship
to academic institutions might taint its claim to an avant-garde practice.
Golding, wisely, dismisses such a position: "criticism of Language writing's
assimilation into the academy rests on an impossible, ahistorical wish for
an ideologically pure, uncontaminated avant-garde that successfully resists
cooption by the institution that it attacks—the wish, perhaps for a radical
otherness outside all considerations of 'canon' " (147).

In fact, as Golding notes, Language writers, as a result of a series of
collaborative activities, stand a good chance of making an effective and
perhaps enduring institutional intervention: "The Language writers' commitment to various forms of group collaboration in a self-reinforcing network of little magazines, small presses, talk series, and reading series . . .
gives their institutional intervention more force: in Silliman's words, 'aesthetic practice raised to an institutional strategy' " (168). Golding, though,
is writing a history, and he attempts to cling to a critical impartiality. Thus,
he uses the abstract "one" to pose a specific challenge to Language writing: "But one can also argue that the next step after establishing a set of
counterinstitutions is to go beyond preaching to the converted and inter-
vene in mainstream institutions" (169). Even when he couches his thought
as a hypothetical possibility—"Language writing may gain its ideological impact, and its long-term effects on American poetry, out of its very
assimilation into the institutions that govern poetry" (170)—Golding, I
believe, is correct in the hints that he drops. As an individual committed
to such institutional interventions, I am more direct. I would (among sev-

eral *simultaneous* strategies) like to see Language writing embrace a more (self-)conscious and calculated effort at institutional intervention. To support and sustain an ongoing poetics of innovation will require savvy institutional strategies. To date, two of the most effective institutional activities are the Poetics Program at the State University of New York, College at Buffalo (with its proliferation of independent presses and journals, the Electronic Poetry Center, and an active reading series) and the publication of volume one of Jerome Rothenberg and Pierre Joris's (1995) *Poems for the Millennium*. It is my sense, however, that more sustained attention must be given to *textbook*-anthologies, like *Understanding Poetry*, which might facilitate the teaching of new reading methods for poetry to a broad range of students and teachers.

The issue of institutional intervention is complex. At a time when many institutionally entrenched poets and critics are beginning to lament and concede the successful incursion into the academy of what might broadly be called "the other tradition," it remains important to assess the complexity of this historical phase. One might imagine, from a position of either enthusiasm or resignation, that we are witnessing that moment of rapid change in taste that Gertrude Stein hypothesizes in "Composition as Explanation," her lucid explanatory lecture delivered at Cambridge and Oxford on 4 June and 7 June 1926. It is easy to imagine that when Charles Bernstein's poetry appears in the *American Poetry Review* (and my own long essay on his work also appears in the *American Poetry Review* [1995]), when a number of works of criticism appear from "major" academic presses, and when the first volume of Jerome Rothenberg and Pierre Joris's monumental anthology *Poems for the Millennium* is published by the University of California Press, that we are seeing that sudden shift which Stein delineates in her 1926 lecture. Perhaps we might think that we are viewing a moment when the artist of, in Stein's words, "the new composition" goes—"there is hardly a moment in between"—from being an "outlaw" to being a "classic." As Stein (1993) details the process, "For a very long time, everybody refuses [the new composition] and then almost without a pause almost everybody accepts. In the history of the refused in the arts and literature the rapidity of the change is always startling" (496).

I find such a vision to be romantic and politically naive, focusing attention *away* from the key mediating institution of the academy. As Golding and Rasula's books demonstrate, the academy is a complex and multifaceted institution. Golding, in a more finely nuanced understanding of "the academy," warns, "First, a distinction should be made between the address, reception, and use of Language writing on the one hand and the institutional status of individuals on the other. To be specific: relatively few Language writers make a full-time living in English departments, and even fewer are employed as *poets*, to teach creative writing. Second, 'assimilation' is a matter of degrees" (148). Golding notes that "even in 1994, only four of the twenty poets in Douglas Messerli's *"Language" Poetries: An Anthology* (1987) are full-time literary academics in tenured or tenure-track positions" (205). Golding's observations hint at the difficulties inherent in any flat reference to "the university" or "the academy" or even to "English departments." All of these entities are undergoing significant changes due to serious budget cuts, reorganization, and the changing nature of employment within the university.

Within most English departments, there is a sharp division between creative writing and the academic sector. While many English departments are in the midst of significant structural and conceptual changes, Jed Rasula's observation may be quite accurate: "but unlike the English departments that generally house them, creative writing programs have doggedly claimed diplomatic immunity from disciplinary reconfiguration" (419). As I argued in Chapter 1, Language writers (and many other innovative poets) present a paradigm of the writer *contrary* to the academic inscription of a fixed boundary (of appointments, teaching duties, and accredited writing for tenure, promotion, and compensation) between creative and "uncreative" (or critical and/or philosophical) writing. Without significant changes in the disciplinary structures of host academic institutions, the overall effect of Language writing and other poetries of "the other tradition" may be minimized, contained, or simply made marginal or anomalous.

The changing nature of the academic job market also mitigates against significant institutional change even if a number of writers from "the other tradition" were to be "absorbed" by the academy. Many full-time tenure-track positions are being eliminated and redistributed in the form of lower-paying temporary positions with heavier teaching loads. The kind of comfortable institutional support of poets that (along with the proliferation of creative writing programs) developed from the late 1950s on into the early 1980s — a situation that caused a number of critics to worry about the literary consequences for a generation of writers so comfortably ensconced — is no longer the situation. The norm today for "emerging" writers is (if anything is available) a low-paying, part-time, temporary position. As an academic administrator, I have seen over the past five years a significant increase in a newly developing tier of academic labor: lecturers, instructors, one-semester and one-year visiting appointments, and by-the-course part-time-temporary instructorships. I mention this economic squeeze of the mid-1990s because it will act to limit the impact that practitioners of innovative poetries will have on the academy: few (new) writers will achieve a secure enough position within the academy to risk engaging in advocacy of significant disciplinary change.

As I argue throughout *Issues and Institutions*, especially in Chapter 3 where I discuss the politics of form, there is most definitely a politics *of* poetry: of its institutional locations, of its formal relationships to readers, of its networks of publication and distribution, of its institutional support (through jobs, prizes, readings, and other forms of subsidy), of its mechanisms of review and recognition, and so on. As Rasula (1995) claims, there are significant political dimensions to "be found intrinsic to its [poetry's] own arena of action. . . . [T]here is, in fact, more than politics *in* the poem; there is also a politics *of* poetry, and this is what language poets have largely chosen to address from the outset" (391).

As Language writing gains an ambiguous toe-hold in an admittedly resistant and already bifurcated academic setting, it remains critical for language writers to become self-reflective about their own politics of poetry. Language writing and other communities of innovative poets have established many productive networks *outside* of academia: numerous independent presses, electronic journals and discussion groups, a proliferation of (hard copy) journals, reading series, CD recordings, and anthologies. Earlier I cited the example of the New Criticism. While decidedly of a different ideology, poetics, and praxis, the history of New Criticism, particularly its enduring effects on poetry pedagogy (at *all* levels), remains instructive for any group interested in creating an enduring institutional presence. At present, Language writing and other poetic practices within the broad terrain of "the other tradition" lack the specific element that proved so effective for New Criticism: an exemplary textbook-anthology that offers a systematic case-study approach to reading and teaching. One problem (addressed in Chapter 7) is that even the current wave of anthologies present innovative poetic practice in isolation and without any attempt to offer significant (alternative) reading methodologies. As Rasula notes of the new anthologies: "none of them attempt to conceive of heterogeneity from outside their own partisan coordinates. . . . Perhaps the surest proof of the institutional dereliction of poetry is that anthologies have consistently failed to 'teach the conflicts,' which in Gerald Graff's view dogs academia as a whole" (465–66).

My own hope would be for a heterogeneous textbook-anthology that would seriously engage the possibility of putting forward alternative methods of reading poetry. At times, I think that such an intervention represents the best hope for breaking the stranglehold of a persistent theme-based conception of reading and understanding poetry. Perhaps such a textbook could point toward a variety of questions and approaches to poetry, thus leaving the notion of a reading methodology open to persistent questioning and development. In the same manner that recent editions of "classic" texts have highlighted conflicting critical approaches, a heterogeneous textbook-anthology focused on conflicting reading methods (and, thus, on alternative modes of *constructing* meaning) might make more audible the vast range of twentieth-century poetics that lies outside the formulas of New Criticism.

Perhaps what I am suggesting begins to sound a bit like Gertrude Stein's (1993) combined lament and hope voiced in 1926: "it is so very much more exciting and satisfactory for everybody if one can have contemporaries, if all one's contemporaries could be one's contemporaries" (496). But the fragmentation of poetry communities in the United States over the past twenty-five years makes such a quest sound ridiculously utopian and naive. Instead of hoping to have "all one's contemporaries" as one's contemporaries, I would gladly settle for an environment of reading, writing, and discussing poetry that allowed many more of one's contemporaries to be one's contemporaries.

I conclude with what might seem like a self-undercutting line of questioning. In a remark that could be easily located in many other sources, Alan Golding acknowledges that "what is in fact the main audience for poetry today [is] the academy" (159). But I wonder if that is any longer the case, even with the large numbers associated with creative writing programs and college courses in contemporary literature. Maria Damon's groundbreaking work *At the Dark End of the Street: Margins in American Poetry Vanguards* (1993), Dana Gioia's "Notes Toward a New Bohemia" (1993), and the many (principally urban) poetry series, independent workshops, and independent publishing ventures may point to a change in venue that, typically, academia may be slow to recognize. Clearly, though, the concentration of *capital* remains vested in the institutions of official verse culture, including the academy. But perhaps a simple addition of the many audiences unaffiliated with academia may provide evidence of a more significant, numerous, and generative base than anyone within academia may yet realize. A more detailed, statistical (and material) study of this nonacademic audience would be of great value.

Since my comments in *Issues and Institutions* tend to be broad in nature, I invite readers interested in more focused, text-specific readings to press on to *Readings*, the second volume of *Opposing Poetries*.

Notes

Chapter 1. Criticism and the Crisis in American Poetry

1. Simpson (1987), 13. Also in Simpson (1986), 3. Other works cited in this chapter are Altieri (1984); Bernstein (1986); Breslin (1984); de Man (1983); Eshleman (1985), 153–57; Fredman (1983); Hall (1983), 90–104; Hass (1984); Kinzie (1984), 63–79; Lyotard (1984); Smith (1985); Stitt (1985); Williamson (1984).

2. When I first wrote this chapter in 1985, I had in mind particularly the many books published by The Figures, Sun and Moon, Tuumba, and North Point, especially Ronald Johnson and Michael Palmer; the writing of David Antin and John Cage; magazines such as *Poetics Journal, Hills, Sulfur, L=A=N=G=U=A=G=E, The Difficulties, Jimmy & Lucy's House of "K,"* and *Paper Air*; the talks and readings at Saint Mark's Church, New York City, and 80 Langton Street, San Francisco; the new series of books from Southern Illinois University Press: *The L=A=N=G=U=A=G=E Book* (Andrews and Bernstein 1984); *Writing/Talks* (Perelman 1985); and *Total Syntax* (Watten 1985); the work of Laura (Riding) Jackson, Rachel Blau DuPlessis, Lyn Hejinian, Judy Grahn, Audre Lorde; and the magazine *How(ever)*.

3. In 1986, at the time of the publication of Bernstein's *Content's Dream*, he had published ten books of poetry. In 1994, with the publication of *Dark City*, Bernstein has now published twenty books of poetry. Sadly, the argument that I was making in 1985 — that Bernstein's work would be, if read and considered, of great value to an institutionalized poetry culture and to discussions of the premises of poetry — remains essentially true today in 1994. In spite of the fact that Bernstein has now published twenty books of poetry, received a Guggenheim Fellowship, holds an endowed chair at the State University of New York at Buffalo, and has had his poetry translated into and discussed in many languages and cultures, his poems do not, for example, appear in any of the "major" anthologies of American Literature, while the poems of many of his contemporaries working within the parameters of "the scenic mode" *do* continue to find substantial representation in these anthologies and in other representations of the variety of American poetry.

4. I again state that my choice (in 1985) of detailed attention to Bernstein's ten-year collection of essays is both representative *and* somewhat arbitrary. There is a large body of literature that would just as easily refute the notion that all is quiet on the Western front. I offer the following list: Watten (1985; especially chaps. 2 and 3, "The Politics of Poetry" and "Total Syntax: The Work of the World"); the first five issues of *Poetics Journal* (especially no. 3: Poetry and Philosophy); *Writing/Talks*, Perelman (1985, particularly the talks by Robert Gluck, Bob Perelman, Ron Silliman, and Lyn Hejinian); writing by Alan Golding on canon formation;

essays by Jed Rasula (some of which are to be found in Andrews and Bernstein 1984); Jackson Mac Low (1982); Marjorie Perloff (1984a; 1984b); Davidson and the work of Ron Silliman (1987). Since distribution and availability are often cited as problems with alternative press publications, let me recommend a general supplier: Small Press Distribution, 1814 San Pablo Avenue, Berkeley, California 94702. I give this specific information because I share Bernstein's (1986) belief that "critics and theorists have the same need to consider contemporary writing techniques as cartographers or economists or sociologists have to consider methodological changes in their field" (381).

Chapter 3. Poetry Readings and the Contemporary Canon

1. This essay was originally delivered, in a slightly different version, on December 28, 1988 as part of a session on "Twentieth-Century American Poetry: Issues in Canon Formation" at the 1988 MLA Convention in New Orleans.

2. For this essay, I am intentionally limiting my attention to university-sponsored readings. Other reading series may often be considerably more diverse. I focus on university-sponsored readings because of their economic impact and their obvious role in canon formation.

3. As Ron Silliman (1987) notes in "The Political Economy of Poetry," by 1926 Laura Riding was complaining about "the forced professionalization of poetry" (21). In part, my own critique of the poetry reading is also a complaint directed against the narrowly conceived professionalization of poetry as practiced in the academy.

4. I selected the 60 colleges to be included in my survey on several bases: (1) colleges selected represented a broad geographical distribution — twenty-nine different states and all regions of the country were included; (2) a substantial number of both public and private institutions were represented; and (3) programs known nationally either for programs in Creative Writing or Ph.D. programs in English were represented.

5. For a slightly different approach to this issue of aesthetic bias in funding decisions, I refer readers to Douglas Messerli's letter in *Poetry Flash* 192 (March 1989): 21. Messerli presents an important argument about NEA biases in the funding of publications.

6. I suspect that a number of readers might wish to dispute the claim that *Tree* poets are midcareer, or even well established at all. However, as Ron Silliman points out, "the *Tree* poets have published at least 280 books between them (the 44 New American poets [Donald Allen 1960 anthology], at the time of the publication of the Allen anthology, had published 125)" (Letter to author, 9 January 1989).

7. Information regarding the NEA's applications and deliberations for the

1988–89 residency and reading programs was provided to me by one of the NEA's panelists, who read applications and made decisions for the 1988–89 round of grant applications. This panelist was able to provide me with detailed lists of proposed poets (for 1988–89), as well as the lists of names from previous reading series and residencies at the applying institutions. As with the data which I have collected, these data too are not exact. For example, I cannot give a precise accounting of which poets finally were funded.

8. My own survey yields essentially the same results. Those poets who gave four or more readings at the universities that responded to my survey were Louise Gluck (6), Jorie Graham (4), Seamus Heaney (4), Sharon Olds (5), Robert Pinsky (5), Derek Walcott (6), and C. K. Williams (5).

9. I am grateful to Alan Golding and Ron Silliman for their careful, skeptical readings of this essay in an earlier form and for their many suggestions for its improvement.

Chapter 5. Experimentation and Politics

1. I dedicate this chapter to the memory of Leland Hickman, poet and editor, who died on 12 May 1991. From 1985 to 1989, Hickman edited and published *Temblor*. This chapter was first delivered (in a slightly different form) as an address at the 1991 American Library Association convention to the ACRL English and American Literature Discussion Group, 1 July 1991. I thank Loss Glazier, Lockwood Library, State University of New York, College at Buffalo, for the invitation.

2. Compare press runs of 400 to 1,000 with the statistics provided in the latest edition of *The Bowker Annual: Library and Book Trade Almanac: 1990–91*: There are 4,607 academic libraries in the United States; 3,376 of these are university and college libraries. The Association of Research Libraries (which includes Canadian libraries) numbers 119. It is obvious that the purchasing plans of academic libraries, especially in relation to the limited output of small presses, have a significant financial impact.

3. See Schmidt (1991). Interestingly enough, Schmidt argues, "Much of what acquisitions librarians wanted added to the curriculum would be useful components to any librarian's education: *a working knowledge of the publishing industry, budgeting techniques, and negotiating business contracts*" (21; my emphasis).

4. I am unable to locate the kind of specific data that would represent the current purchasing habits of university and college libraries. Available statistical information is not broken down into book-purchases by kind of press (i.e., trade press versus small press) nor by genre. Nevertheless, I do believe that such data, broken down by percentages and dollar amounts, would support my argument that library purchase plans of poetry greatly overemphasize trade and university press publications.

Chapter 6. Thinking Made in the Mouth

1. For a more detailed discussion of the relationship between reading habits and characterizations of contemporary American poetry, see Chapter 1.

2. See, for example, Nelson 1989 and Perloff 1984a, 1985, 1986, and 1990.

3. Of course such immediacy of the word need not be tied to the predominance of the oral qualities of poetry. The poetry of Steve McCaffery, Hannah Weiner, Susan Howe, Tina Darragh, John Byrum, Dick Higgins, and Stephen-Paul Martin is rich in examples of textual presence achieved by print-oriented strategies and by making adventurous use of the page as a unit of composition.

4. For a detailed discussion of the politics of form and its relationship to issues of self-representation, see Chapter 4.

5. For example, when Antin presented a talk-poem, "black warrior," at the University of Alabama in 1990, virtually no one from the English department or creative writing faculties would speak to him after the talk. Members of the art department, undergraduates, and other graduate students, however, were much less threatened by and receptive to Antin's performance.

6. Doty's (1986) description of mythography, though not intended as such, serves as an excellent description of Antin's talk-poem "talking at the boundaries," particularly the talk's conclusion where Antin focuses on the moral choices confronting a young Marine.

7. My own interactions with David Antin over the past five or so years are consistent with his vision of a community of artists. His own layout of the talk-poems, which I think of as *phrasal*, has been crucial to my own writing practice. That method, as well as his remarks on collage, have led me to dedicate my book of poems *INTER(IR)RUPTIONS* (1992) to David Antin.

8. For a discussion of conventions and institutional politics of the poetry reading, see Chapter 3.

9. Such a declaration, it must be noted, applies as well to Antin's recomposition of his talk-poems for inclusion in book publications. That is, just as Antin's performances honor the present, so too does his act of transcription. Antin will revise, add, and delete as he honors a different present moment of poesis in the act of transcribing a previously presented talk-poem. In the tapes which Antin has made available to me, the most noteworthy difference is in the ending to "talking at the boundaries," where the Marine's story on tape is much more rambling than the transcribed version.

10. As I had imagined before I had the chance to see Antin do a talk-poem live, Antin does engage in considerable preparation prior to a performance. The nature of that preparation seems to involve a meditative consideration of what particular narratives and questions engage Antin at the moment or period of performance, as well as some thought about which narratives and stories might be juxtaposed. Antin does not work from written notes.

11. For a more detailed consideration of these claims, see Chapter 3.

12. As a personal and pedagogical aside, which verifies Rothenberg's contentions, I recently began a graduate seminar in poetics (where our main objects of study were the writings of Thoreau and Dickinson) by presenting for discussion a Navajo coyote song which is transcribed simply as a set of transliterated sounds/syllables on page 8 of Rothenberg's *Technicians of the Sacred* (1985). I found especially illuminating the way in which this text immediately removed both my customary authority and the class's habitual modes of generating discussion. That is, the removal of the possibility of immediately directing a discussion to issues of theme and meaning led us in other directions, simultaneously exposing our usually unspoken presuppositions about what to do with poems and focusing our attention on ways in which sound itself (nearly apart from sense) communicates.

13. Such a description calls to mind Michael Oakeshott's (1962) and Kenneth Burke's (1973) independent elaborations of philosophy as a form of extended conversation.

14. It should, however, be noted that Antin does not engage in a flat idealization of orality's seeming immediacy over the seeming erasure of labor and immediacy in the book. The best discussion of the dialectical relationship between speech and writing that Antin works out of can be found in Sayre 1982.

15. I have intentionally devoted a good deal of my attention to relatively recent talk-poems by Antin. I do so because in these talk-poems Antin's reflections on narrative as well as on issues of belief and exile (which I take up later) are most explicit. A number of these talk-poems are published in Antin (1993). I thank David Antin for making many of these talk-poems available to me and for discussing them with me.

16. Note that though earlier in "The Price" Antin had rather snidely dismissed the merits of French deconstruction, here he is engaged in a vernacular philosophizing both compatible with Derridean notions of *différance* and informed by such theorizing. I find it interesting that especially theoretically sophisticated academics who listen to Antin's talk-poems often fail to perceive that his humorous dismissal of theory masks his own vernacular and story-based participation in the same issues. When Antin presented "black warrior" at the University of Alabama (April 5, 1990), many theorists in the audience could not get past Antin's opening jabs at French deconstruction long enough to realize that his own thinking—and Antin is well-read in linguistics, rhetoric, and philosophy, and has had close working relationships with French theorists such as Michel de Certeau, who was in residence for quite some time at the University of California, San Diego, where Antin teaches—participates in current theoretical issues but by means of a different vocabulary and methodology. Antin's is a thinking poesis that is open to "high" and "low" discourses, and it is a thinking poesis rich in anecdotal material. Thus Antin's work stands as a critique and an accusation of professionalized behavior in poetry, philosophy, and critical theory.

17. Perhaps it is that supposed distance from writing that leads to a common criticism of Rothenberg's poetry generally and especially of the total translations: such poetry is not accessible for a reader who only has the printed page to consider. While I think there is a small element of truth to the complaint—obviously access to Rothenberg reading/singing the poems *is* helpful—the implication that the poems are somehow "not successful" if they are not immediately accessible as written texts is a presupposition worth investigating. Such a presupposition depends on narrow assumptions about "reading," kinds of valued and professionalized forms of "meaning," and an implied version of mastery in reading. A Rothenberg total translation, even for a reader who has never heard Rothenberg sing the poem, offers an important and productive occasion for the reader to sound the poem (aloud!), to participate in the making of sounds, to learn about poetry's potentials and actualities by speaking/singing. Such pedagogy and experience is very much in keeping with the title of this chapter, "Thinking Made in the Mouth." It is not a form of thinking that appeals to readers bent on reading as a form of confirmation of presupposed certainties; instead, it is a thinking that confirms processes, sounding, and questioning.

18. Poem 1144, p. 512, in Thomas H. Johnson (1955), and Letter 750, 30 April 1882, p. 279, in Thomas H. Johnson (1986).

19. Oddly enough, in 1990 at an international conference sponsored by *Tikkun*, the panel on contemporary Jewish poetry consisted of Antin, Rothenberg, and Marjorie Perloff, all of whom can be seen as Jews whose identities as Jews have very much to do with faith and doubt, exile, and an anti-essentialist view of ethnicity. Antin's talk-poem "Writing and Exile," performed at the conference, appears in *Tikkun*; see Antin (1990).

20. Bernstein's interpretation of Jewish identity applies equally well to Bernstein's own writing and to the work of a number of other similarly Jewish writers, including Rachel Blau DuPlessis, Edmond Jabès, Jacques Derrida, David Antin, myself, David Ignatow, Adrienne Rich, and others. It can be argued that such indirection of identity, especially in representing the divine, has certain affinities with Orthodox Judaism (and prohibitions against direct images or names for the divine).

21. For a better sense of Rothenberg's complex Jewish refusals and identities, see Rothenberg 1978, and his two books of poetry, Rothenberg 1974 and 1989.

Chapter 7. Anthologies, Poetry, and Postmodernism

1. In this chapter I refer mainly to Lauter (1994), Messerli (1994), and Hoover (1994). Two other recent poetry anthologies of note are Weinberger (1993) and Barone and Ganick (1994).

2. While I am highly critical of the Heath anthology, especially as it relates to twentieth-century American poetry, I have immense respect for Lauter's overall project. In fact, I have taught from the Heath for several years, and I advocated (successfully) its adoption at the University of Alabama for core courses in American Literature. The competing American Literature anthologies that I have in mind are the Norton (4th ed., 1993), HarperCollins (2d ed., 1993), Prentice-Hall (1991), and McGraw-Hill (8th ed., 1994). As I go on to say several times in this essay, all of the anthologies (by themselves) are unfit for teaching the range and intensity of conflicting assumptions and practices in contemporary American poetry. My own choice as a teacher (for fall 1994 in a graduate course in American Poetry since World War II) has been to teach side by side two anthologies, Messerli (1994) and A. Poulin (1985), along with several individual books of poetry.

3. For a more detailed treatment of the relationship between multiculturalism and innovation, see Chapter 4. The quote from the Heath anthology also raises the question, What makes a literature "new"? A "new" writer? "New" subject matter? A "new" form?

4. As for the term "postmodern" itself, Hoover (1994) begins with Charles Olson's "first" use of the term postmodern:

> The poet Charles Olson used the word "postmodern" as early as an October 20, 1951, letter to Creeley from Black Mountain, North Carolina. Doubting the value of historical relics when compared with the process of living, Olson states: "And had we not, ourselves (I mean postmodern man), better just leave such things behind us — and not so much trash of discourse, & gods?" (xxv)

Though Hoover cites Olson, Olson certainly was not the first to use this term. As Mazzaro (1980, viii) points out, Randall Jarrell, for example, first used the term postmodern in regard to American poetry in a 1946 review of Robert Lowell's *Lord Weary's Castle*. There are, admittedly, several overlapping and imprecise terms that may be employed: postmodern, avant-garde, experimental, innovative. Of the three editors, Hoover does the best job of explaining his choice of terms and his decision to use the term "postmodern":

> Over the years the term has received increasing acceptance in all areas of culture and the arts; it has even come to be considered a reigning style. As used here, "postmodern" means the historical period following World War II. It also suggests an experimental approach to composition, as well as a worldview that sets itself apart from mainstream culture and the narcissism, sentimentality, and self-expressiveness of its life in writing. Postmodernist poetry is the avant-garde poetry of our time. I have chosen "postmodern" for the title over "experimental" and "avant garde" because it is the most encompassing term for

the variety of experimental practice since World War II, one that ranges from the oral poetics of Beat and performance poetries to the more "writerly" work of the New York School and language poetry. (xxv)

While many academic debates over postmodernism pivot about Fredric Jameson's much-heralded 1984 essay "Postmodernism, or the Cultural Logic of Late Capitalism" the concept and the term postmodernism had already been given a sustained and provocative treatment in David Antin's extraordinary 1972 essay "Modernism and Postmodernism: Approaching the Present in American Poetry." In addition to offering a challenging view of modernism and postmodernism, Antin warns us of the extraordinary difficulty of representing the present:

> Clearly the sense that such a thing as a "postmodern" sensibility exists and should be defined is wrapped up with the conviction that what we have called "modern" for so long is thoroughly over. If we are capable of imagining the "modern" as a closed set of stylistic features, "modern" can no longer mean present. For it is precisely the distinctive feature of the present that, in spite of any strong sense of its coherence, it is always open on its forward side. (98–99)

5. As an aside, one consequence of my survey of current anthologies is a deep conviction that the shortcomings of these anthologies serve to point out the exceptional nature of the thirty years of anthology-projects by Jerome Rothenberg—particularly *Shaking the Pumpkin* (1972), *America a Prophecy* (Quasha and Rothenberg 1974), and *Technicians of the Sacred* (1968, 1985). (Rothenberg, along with Pierre Joris, is currently completing a two-volume anthology of twentieth century poetry; see Rothenberg and Joris 1995). While even the Hoover and Messerli anthologies, and especially all of the American Literature anthologies, fall prey to an unreflective, habit-worn conceptualization of the anthology and the book, Rothenberg's anthology-work, from the very beginning, has been innovative and fresh. For example, the Heath's "bold" move of integrating American Literature with Native American material and with exploration narratives was already fully accomplished in Quasha and Rothenberg (1974). The somewhat innovative acceptance of visual poetries in Messerli (1994) was already presented in Quasha and Rothenberg (1974), where, for example, the mound constructions of southern Ohio Native Americans stand as a kind of visual or concrete poetry beside Hopi poems and poems by William Cullen Bryant.

6. Perhaps the dominance of *Understanding Poetry* (Brooks and Warren 1938) as an academic textbook can be explained, in part, precisely because as a textbook it offered many detailed examples of the kinds of reading and critical responses advocated by Brooks and Warren.

7. Special thanks to the Poetics Group (POETICS@UBVM.CC.BUFFALO.EDU) participants. A lively discussion (June–August 1994) of the new anthologies proved stimulating and instructive for the writing of this essay.

Works Cited

Allen, Donald. 1960. *The New American Poetry*. New York: Grove.

Altieri, Charles. 1984. *Self and Sensibility in Contemporary American Poetry*. Cambridge: Cambridge University Press.

Andrews, Bruce. 1990. "Poetry as Explanation, Poetry as Praxis." In *The Politics of Poetic Form: Poetry and Public Policy*, edited by Charles Bernstein. New York: Roof Books.

Andrews, Bruce, and Charles Bernstein, eds. 1984. *The L=A=N=G=U=A=G=E Book*. Carbondale: Southern Illinois University Press.

Antin, David. 1972. "Modernism and Postmodernism: Approaching the Present in American Poetry." *Boundary 2*, vol. 1, no. 1:98–133.

———. 1976. *Talking at the Boundaries*. New York: New Directions.

———. 1984. *Tuning*. New York: New Directions.

———. 1985. "what it means to be avant-garde." *Formations* 2, no. 2:53–71.

———. 1989. "The Price." *Representations* 28:14–33.

———. 1990. "Writing and Exile." *Tikkun* 5, no. 5:47–52.

———. 1993. *What it Means to be Avant-Garde*. New York: New Directions.

Barone, Dennis, and Peter Ganick. 1994. *The Art of Practice: 45 Contemporary Poets*. Elmwood, Conn.: Potes & Poets Press.

Barthes, Roland. 1975. *The Pleasure of the Text*. New York: Hill and Wang.

Bernstein, Charles. 1980. *Controlling Interests*. New York: Roof Books.

———. 1983. *Islets/Irritations*. New York: Jordan Davies. Repr., New York: Roof Books, 1992.

———. 1986. *Content's Dream: Essays, 1975–1984*. Los Angeles: Sun & Moon Press.

———. 1987. *Artifice of Absorption*. Philadelphia: Singing Horse Press/Paper Air. Repr. in *A Poetics*, by Charles Bernstein. Cambridge: Harvard University Press, 1992.

———. 1990. *The Politics of Poetic Form: Poetry and Public Policy*. New York: Roof Books.

———. 1992. *A Poetics*. Cambridge: Harvard University Press.

———. 1994. *Dark City*. Los Angeles: Sun & Moon Press.

Breslin, James E. B. 1984. *From Modern to Contemporary: American Poetry, 1945–1965*. Chicago: University of Chicago Press.

Brooks, Cleanth, and Robert Penn Warren, eds. 1938. *Understanding Poetry*. New York: Henry Holt. 3d ed., 1960.

Burke, Kenneth. 1973. *The Philosophy of Literary Form: Studies in Symbolic Action*. 3d ed. Berkeley and Los Angeles: University of California Press.

Coffey, Michael. 23 November 1990. "Schiffrin Says 'Corporatization' Shrinks Book Trade Choices." *Publishers Weekly* 237:14.

Damon, Maria. 1993. *At the Dark End of the Street: Margins in American Poetry Vanguards.* Minneapolis: University of Minnesota Press.

Davidson, Michael. "Notes on Writing and Production." *Paper Air* 3, no. 1.

de Man, Paul. 1983. *Blindness and Insight: Essays in the Rhetoric of Contemporary Criticism.* 2d rev. ed. Minneapolis: University of Minnesota Press.

Doty, William G. 1986. *Mythography: The Study of Myths and Rituals.* Tuscaloosa: University of Alabama Press.

———, ed. 1995. *Picturing Cultural Values in Postmodern America.* Tuscaloosa: University of Alabama Press.

DuPlessis, Rachel Blau. 1987. *Tabula Rosa.* Elmwood, Conn.: Potes & Poets Press.

Eshleman, Clayton. 1985. "Response to Mary Kinzie." *Sulfur* 13:153–57.

Foley, Jack. 1993. *Adrift.* Berkeley, Calif.: Pantograph.

Fredman, Stephen. 1983. *Poet's Prose: The Crisis in American Verse.* Cambridge: Cambridge University Press.

Gioia, Dana. May 1991. "Can Poetry Matter?" *Atlantic Monthly*: 94–106.

———. 1993. "Notes toward a New Bohemia." *Poetry Flash* 248:7, 13, 14.

Golding, Alan. 1984. "A History of American Poetry Anthologies." In *Canons,* edited by Robert von Hallberg. Chicago: University of Chicago Press.

———. 1995. *From Outlaw to Classic: Canons in American Poetry.* Madison: University of Wisconsin Press.

Hall, Donald. 1983. "Poetry and Ambition." *Kenyon Review*: 90–104.

———. 1987. "Poetry and Ambition." In *What Is a Poet? Essays from the Eleventh Alabama Symposium on English and American Literature,* edited by Hank Lazer. Tuscaloosa: University of Alabama Press.

Harris, Marie, and Kathleen Aguero, eds. 1987. *A Gift of Tongues: Critical Challenges in Contemporary American Poetry.* Athens: University of Georgia Press.

———, eds. 1989. *An Ear to the Ground: An Anthology of Contemporary American Poetry.* Athens: University of Georgia Press.

Hartley, George. 1989. *Textual Politics and the Language Poets.* Bloomington: Indiana University Press.

Hass, Robert. 1984. *Twentieth-Century Pleasures: Prose on Poetry.* New York: Ecco Press.

Heidegger, Martin. 1971. "What Are Poets For?" In his *Poetry, Language, Thought,* translated and with an Introduction by Albert Hofstadter. New York: Harper and Row.

Hejinian, Lyn. 1978. *Writing is an Aid to Memory.* Great Barrington, Mass.: The Figures.

———. 1987. *My Life.* Los Angeles: Sun & Moon Press.

Hoover, Paul, ed. 1994. *Postmodern American Poetry.* New York: Norton.

Jabès, Edmond. 1976–84. *The Book of Questions.* Translated by Rosmarie
Waldrop. Middletown: Wesleyan University Press.

Jameson, Fredric. 1984. "Postmodernism, or the Cultural Logic of Late
Capitalism." *New Left Review,* no. 146:53–92.

Johnson, Thomas H. 1955. *The Complete Poems of Emily Dickinson.* Boston: Little,
Brown.

———. 1986. *Emily Dickinson: Selected Letters.* Cambridge: Harvard University
Press.

Kalaidjian, Walter. 1989. *Languages of Liberation: The Social Text in Contemporary
American Poetry.* New York: Columbia University Press.

Kinzie, Mary. 1984. "The Rhapsodic Fallacy." *Salmagundi* 65:63–79.

Lauter, Paul. 1991. *Canons and Contexts.* New York: Oxford University Press.

———, ed. 1994. *The Heath Anthology of American Literature.* Vol. 2. 2d ed.
Lexington, Mass.: Heath.

Lazer, Hank. 1984. "Critical Theory and Contemporary American Poetry."
Missouri Review 3, no. 3:246–65.

———. 1986. "Criticism and the Crisis in American Poetry." *Missouri Review*
7:201–32.

———. 1987. *What Is a Poet? Essays from the Eleventh Alabama Symposium on
English and American Literature.* Tuscaloosa: University of Alabama Press.

———. 1990a. "Poetry Readings and the Contemporary Canon." *American
Poetry* 7, no. 2:64–72.

———. 1990b. "The Politics of Form and Poetry's Other Subjects: Reading
Contemporary American Poetry." *American Literary History* 2, no. 3:503–27.

———. 1992. *INTER(IR)RUPTIONS.* Mentor, Ohio: Generator.

———. 1995. "Charles Bernstein's *Dark City*: Polis, Policy, and the Policing of
Poetry." *American Poetry Review* 24 (September–October): 35–44.

———. 1996. *Readings.* Vol. 2 of *Opposing Poetries.* Evanston: Northwestern
University Press.

Levertov, Denise. 1981. *Light Up The Cave.* New York: New Directions.

Lyotard, Jean-François. 1984. *The Postmodern Condition: A Report on Knowledge.*
Minneapolis: University of Minnesota Press.

Mac Low, Jackson. 1982. "Language Centered." $L=A=N=G=U=A=G=E$
4:23–26.

Marcuse, Herbert. 1978. *The Aesthetic Dimension: Toward a Critique of Marxist
Aesthetics.* Boston: Beacon.

Martin, Stephen-Paul. 1988. *Open Form and the Feminine Imagination: The
Politics of Reading in Twentieth-Century Innovative Writing.* Washington, D.C.:
Maisonneuve Press.

Mazzaro, Jerome. 1980. *Postmodern American Poetry.* Champaign: University of
Illinois Press.

McCaffery, Steve. 1986. *North of Intention: Critical Writings, 1973–1986*. New York: Roof Books; Toronto: Nightwood Editions.

McClatchy, J. D. 1989. *White Paper: On Contemporary American Poetry*. New York: Columbia University Press.

McGann, Jerome. 1987. "Language Writing." *London Review of Books* 9 (15 October): 6–8.

Messerli, Douglas, ed. 1987. *"Language" Poetries: An Anthology*. New York: New Directions.

———. 1988. *Maxims from My Mother's Milk/Hymns to Him: A Dialogue*. Los Angeles: Sun & Moon Press.

———, ed. 1994. *From the Other Side of the Century: A New American Poetry, 1960–1990*. Los Angeles: Sun & Moon Press.

Nelson, Cary. 1981. *Our Last First Poets: Vision and History in Contemporary American Poetry*. Urbana: University of Illinois Press.

———. 1989. *Repression and Recovery: Modern American Poetry and the Politics of Cultural Memory, 1910–1945*. Madison: University of Wisconsin Press.

Oakeshott, Michael Joseph. 1962. "The Voice of Poetry in the Conversation of Mankind." In his *Rationalism in Politics and Other Essays*. New York: Basic Books.

Ott, Gil. 1989. *Public Domain*. Elmwood, Conn.: Potes & Poets Press.

Paul, Sherman. 1986. *In Search of the Primitive: Rereading David Antin, Jerome Rothenberg, and Gary Snyder*. Baton Rouge: Louisiana State University Press.

Perelman, Bob. 1988. "Language Writing and Audience." Paper delivered at the Modern Language Association Conference, 24 December.

———, ed. 1985. *Writing/Talks*. Carbondale: Southern Illinois University Press.

———. 1986. *First World*. Great Barrington, Mass.: The Figures.

Perloff, Marjorie. 1984a. *The Poetics of Indeterminacy: Rimbaud to Cage*. Princeton: Princeton University Press.

———. 1984b. "The Word as Such: $L = A = N = G = U = A = G = E$ Poetry in the Eighties." *American Poetry Review* 13 (May–June): 15–22. Repr. in her *Dance of the Intellect*, 215–38.

———. 1985. *The Dance of the Intellect: Studies in the Poetry of the Pound Tradition*. New York: Cambridge University Press.

———. 1986. *The Futurist Movement: Avant-Garde, Avant Guerre, and the Language of Rupture*. Chicago: University of Chicago Press.

———. 1990. *Poetic License: Essays on Modernist and Postmodernist Lyric*. Evanston: Northwestern University Press.

Pinsky, Robert. 1976. *The Situation of Poetry: Contemporary Poetry and Its Traditions*. Princeton: Princeton University Press.

Poulin, A., Jr. 1985. *Contemporary American Poetry*. 4th ed. Boston: Houghton Mifflin.

Quasha, George, and Jerome Rothenberg, eds. 1974. *America, A Prophecy: A New Reading of American Poetry from Pre-Columbian Times to the Present*. New York: Random House.

Rasula, Jed. 1995. *The American Poetry Wax Museum: Reality Effects, 1940–1990*. Urbana, Ill.: National Council of Teachers of English.

Retallack, Joan. 1993. *Errata 5uite*. Washington, D.C.: Edge Books.

Rothenberg, Jerome. 1968. *Technicians of the Sacred: A Range of Poetries from Africa, America, Asia, and Oceania*. 1st ed. Garden City, N.Y.: Doubleday.

——. 1970. *The 17 Horse Songs of Frank Mitchell, X–XIII*. London: Tetrad Press.

——. 1971. "Recordings of Horse Songs X and XIII." *Alcheringa*, no. 2.

——, ed. 1972. *Shaking the Pumpkin: Traditional Poetry of the Indian North Americas*. New York: Doubleday.

——. 1974. *Poland/1931*. New York: New Directions.

——, ed. 1978. *A Big Jewish Book: Poems and Other Visions of the Jews from Tribal Times to Present*. New York: Doubleday.

——. 1981. *Pre-Faces and Other Writings*. New York: New Directions.

——, ed. 1985. *Technicians of the Sacred: A Range of Poetries from Africa, America, Asia, and Oceania*. 2d ed. Berkeley and Los Angeles: University of California Press.

——. 1989. *Khurbn and Other Poems*. New York: New Directions.

——. 1994. "A Poetics of the Sacred." In *Picturing Cultural Values*, edited by William Doty. Tuscaloosa: University of Alabama Press.

Rothenberg, Jerome, and Pierre Joris, eds. 1995. From *Fin-de-Siècle to Negritude*. Vol. 1 of *Poems for the Millennium: The University of California Book of Modern and Postmodern Poetry*. Berkeley and Los Angeles: University of California Press.

Rothenberg, Jerome, and Diane Rothenberg, eds. 1983. *A Symposium of the Whole: A Range of Discourse toward an Ethnopoetics*. With commentaries by Jerome Rothenberg and Diane Rothenberg. Berkeley and Los Angeles: University of California Press.

Sayre, Henry. 1982. "David Antin and the Oral Poetics Movement." *Contemporary Literature* 23, no. 4:428–50.

——. 1989. *The Object of Performance: The American Avant-Garde Since 1970*. Chicago: University of Chicago Press.

Schmidt, Karen A. 1991. "The Education of the Acquisitions Librarian: A Survey of ARL Acquisitions Librarians." *Library Resources and Technical Services* 35:7–22.

Silliman, Ron. 1978. *Ketjak*. San Francisco: This.

——. 1981. *Tjanting*. Great Barrington, Mass.: The Figures.

——, ed. 1986. *In the American Tree: Language, Realism, Poetry*. Orono:

National Poetry Foundation, University of Maine at Orono.

———. 1987. *The New Sentence*. New York: Roof Books.

———. 1990. "Canons and Institutions: New Hope for the Disappeared." In *The Politics of Poetic Form: Poetry and Public Policy*, edited by Charles Bernstein. New York: Roof Books.

Simpson, Louis Aston Marantz. 1986. "The Character of the Poet." In his *The Character of the Poet*. Ann Arbor: University of Michigan Press.

———. 1987. "The Character of the Poet." In *What Is a Poet? Essays from the Eleventh Alabama Symposium on English and American Literature*, edited by Hank Lazer. Tuscaloosa: University of Alabama Press.

Smith, Dave. 1985. *Local Assays: On Contemporary American Poetry*. Champaign: University of Illinois Press.

Smith, Dave, and David Bottoms, eds. 1985. *The Morrow Anthology of Younger American Poets*. New York: Quill.

Stein, Gertrude. 1962. *Selected Writings of Gertrude Stein*. Edited and with an Introduction and Notes by Carl Van Vechten, and with an essay on Gertrude Stein by F. W. Dupee. New York: Random House, Modern Library.

———. 1993. *A Stein Reader*. Edited and with an Introduction by Ulla E. Dydo. Evanston: Northwestern University Press.

Stevens, Wallace. 1972. *The Palm at the End of the Mind: Selected Poems*. New York: Vintage.

Stitt, Peter. 1985. *The World's Hieroglyphic Beauty: Five American Poets*. Athens: University of Georgia Press.

———. 1987. "Writers, Theorists, and the Department of English." *AWP Newsletter* (September–October): 1–3.

Turner, Victor. 1982. *From Ritual to Theatre: The Human Seriousness of Play*. New York: Performing Arts Journal Publications.

Vendler, Helen. 1985. *The Harvard Book of Contemporary American Poetry*. Cambridge: Belknap Press of Harvard University Press.

Vincent, Stephen, and Ellen Zweig, eds. 1981. *The Poetry Reading: A Contemporary Compendium on Language and Performance*. San Francisco, Calif.: Momo's Press.

von Hallberg, Robert, ed. 1984. *Canons*. Chicago: University of Chicago Press.

———. 1985. *American Poetry and Culture, 1945–1980*. Cambridge: Harvard University Press.

Watten, Barrett. 1985. *Total Syntax*. Carbondale: Southern Illinois University Press.

Weinberger, Eliot. 1993. *American Poetry Since 1950: Innovators and Outsiders*. New York: Marsilio.

Weiner, Hannah. 1984. *Spoke*. Los Angeles: Sun & Moon Press.

Williams, Raymond. 1977. *Marxism and Literature*. Oxford: Oxford University Press.

Williams, William Carlos. 1974. *The Embodiment of Knowledge.* Edited and with an Introduction by Ron Loewinsohn. New York: New Directions.

Williamson, Alan. 1984. *Introspection and Contemporary Poetry.* Cambridge: Harvard University Press.

Index

Adorno, Theodor, 60, 70
Allen, Donald
  New American Poetry, 17, 38, 134, 135
Althusser, Louis, 33
Altieri, Charles, 7, 27, 29, 30, 32, 34, 57
  Self and Sensibility in Contemporary
    American Poetry, 17–25
Alurista, 74, 131
Andrews, Bruce, 40, 63–64, 136
Antin, David, 4, 17, 31, 49, 54, 55, 59,
  67, 71–72, 91–125, 136, 138
  "Modernism and Postmodernism:
    Approaching the Present in
    American Poetry," 94–95
  "The Price," 114–17
  "talking at the boundaries," 99, 117
  Tuning, 113–14
  "What it means to be avant-garde,"
    117
  "Writing and Exile," 122
Ashbery, John, 9, 14–15, 23, 25, 134, 137

Bacon, Francis, 87
Baraka, Amiri, 133
Barthes, Roland, 12, 31
Basho, Matsuo, 12
Bernstein, Charles, 7, 8, 25, 26, 31, 35,
  39, 46, 48, 53–54, 62, 64, 69, 78, 82,
  87–89, 98, 118, 121, 128, 133, 148
  Content's Dream: Essays 1975–1985, 2,
    22–30
  The Politics of Poetic Form: Poetry
    and Public Policy, 63, 65
  "Sentences My Father Used," 42–43,
    45
Berrigan, Ted, 14
Bishop, Elizabeth, 58
Blackburn, Paul, 85
Blake, William, 98

Bloom, Harold, 33, 58, 102
Bly, Robert, 61
Braque, Georges, 35
Breslin, James E. B., 7, 22, 27, 29, 31,
  34, 136
  From Modern to Contemporary:
    American Poetry 1945–1965, 15–18,
    48
Brooks, Cleanth, and Robert Penn
  Warren
  Understanding Poetry, 145, 146, 148,
Brooks, Gwendolyn, 61
Bruce-Novoa, Juan, 74, 76–77
Bruchac, Joseph, 77
Buber, Martin, 124
Burke, Kenneth, 190
Buson, Yosa, 12

Cage, John, 17, 69, 96, 97, 98, 134, 135,
  138
Cárdenas, Reyes, 73, 74
Ceravalo, Joseph, 86
Cerf, Bennett, 83
Cervantes, Lorna Dee, 75, 76
Cézanne, Paul, 35
Cha, Theresa, 60
Cofer, Judith Ortiz, 129, 131
Coleridge, Samuel Taylor, 33
Corman, Cid, 147
Crawford, John, 75–76
Creeley, Robert, 14, 137
Cruz, Victor Hernández, 128
Culler, Jonathan, 70

Dahlen, Beverly, 63
Damon, Maria, 151
Darragh, Tina, 67
  "ludicrous stick," 43–45
Davidson, Michael, 2

de Man, Paul, 18, 25
Derrida, Jacques, 31, 33
Descartes, René, 87
Diamond, Stanley, 123
Dickinson, Emily, 121, 135
Doty, William, 93, 99–100
Drucker, Johanna, 67
Duchamp, Marcel, 35, 95, 98
Duncan, Robert, 33, 134
DuPlessis, Rachel Blau, 63, 73, 147

Eliade, Mircea, 119
Eliot, T.S., 15, 45, 95, 96, 135
Emerson, Ralph Waldo, 96
Eshleman, Clayton, 31–33

Foley, Jack, 137
Foucault, Michel, 33
Fredman, Stephen, 7, 35
    Poet's Prose: The Crisis in American
        Verse, 30–31, 32, 36
Freud, Sigmund, 27, 57
Frost, Robert, 73, 113

Gablik, Suzi, 140
Ginsberg, Allen, 15
Gioia, Dana, 91–92, 137, 151
    "Can Poetry Matter?," 80–81, 89
Golding, Alan
    From Outlaw to Classic: Canons in
        American Poetry, 144–52
Graff, Gerald, 151
Gregerson, Linda, 33
Grenier, Robert, 38

Hall, Donald, 10, 21, 30
Harjo, Joy, 75
Harris, Marie, and Kathleen Aguero
    A Gift of Tongues: Critical Challenges
        in Contemporary American Poetry,
        72–78
    An Ear to the Ground: An Anthology

of Contemporary American Poetry,
    72–78
Harrison, Jane, 108
Harryman, Carla, 60
Hartley, George
    Textual Politics and the Language
        Poets, 60, 61, 65–67, 68, 70, 78
Hass, Robert, 7
    Twentieth Century Pleasures: Prose on
        Poetry, 11–13
Heidegger, Martin, 33
    "What Are Poets For?," 85–86
Hejinian, Lyn, 24, 46, 69
    Writing Is an Aid to Memory, 40–42,
        45
Holden, Jonathan, 19
Holzer, Jenny, 67
Hongo, Garrett, 129–31
Hoover, Paul, 4
    Postmodern American Poetry, 126–43
Howard, Richard, 7
Howe, Susan, 60, 63
Hughes, Langston, 133, 140
Hunt, Erica, 131
Husserl, Edmund, 33

Jabès, Edmond, 82, 122
Jameson, Fredric, 94
Jarrell, Randall, 7, 11
Jordan, June, 75, 133
Jung, Carl, 57

Kafka, Franz, 105, 121
Kalaidjian, Walter
    Languages of Liberation: The Social
        Text in Contemporary American
        Poetry, 60–63, 68, 82–84
Keats, John, 33
Keillor, Garrison, 117
Kierkegaard, Søren, 113
Kinzie, Mary, 34
    The Rhapsodic Fallacy, 31–33

Koolish, Lynda, 75, 76
Kristeva, Julia, 62

Lasch, Christopher, 13
Laska, P. J., 72
Lauter, Paul, 4, 77
  *The Heath Anthology of American
    Literature*, Vol. 2, 2d ed., 126–43
Laviera, Tato, 128
Leiris, Michel, 69
Levertov, Denise, 49
Levine, Philip, 76, 129
Locke, Alain, 133, 140
Lorde, Audre, 75, 133
Lowell, Robert, 14, 58, 72, 113
Lyotard, Jean-François
  *The Postmodern Condition: A Report
    on Knowledge*, 35–36

McAllester, David, 119
McCaffery, Steve, 39, 40, 69
McClatchy, J. D.
  *White Paper: On Contemporary
    American Poetry*, 56–58, 63, 64
McGann, Jerome, 39
Mackey, Nathaniel, 38, 131
Mac Low, Jackson, 25
Major, Clarence, 60
Marcuse, Herbert, 125
Martin, Stephen-Paul
  *Open Form and the Feminine Imagi-
    nation*, 59–60
Marx, Karl, 27, 33
Mazzaro, James, 7
Merleau-Ponty, Maurice, 33
Merwin, W. S., 61–62, 68
Messerli, Douglas
  *From the Other Side of the Century: A
    New American Poetry, 1960–1990*,
    126–43
  "Language" Poetries, 3, 4, 37–46, 149

Milosz, Czeslaw, 13
Mitchell, Frank, 98, 118

Nelson, Cary, 7, 35, 92, 97
Nicol, bp, 132
Nixon, Nicholas, 71

Ohmann, Richard, 145
Olson, Charles, 62, 66, 68, 95, 108–9,
    135, 137, 147
Oppen, George, 68, 134
Oppenheim, Dennis, 70
Ortiz, Simon, 128
Ott, Gil, 88

Paul, Sherman, 95, 99, 109, 120–22
Perelman, Bob, 46, 53, 62, 71
  "Seduced by Analogy," 44, 45
Perloff, Marjorie, 2, 7, 40, 136
  *Poetic License: Essays on Modern and
    Postmodern Lyric*, 67–70, 71, 73,
    78
Picasso, Pablo, 35
Pinsky, Robert
  The Situation of Poetry, 13
Plato, 95
Poulin, A., Jr.
  Contemporary American Poetry, 38
Pound, Ezra, 28, 45, 68, 136

Rasula, Jed
  *The American Poetry Wax Museum:
    Reality Effects*, 144–52
Retallack, Joan, 131–32
Reznikoff, Charles, 134
Rich, Adrienne, 19, 62, 133, 137
Rothenberg, Jerome, 4, 33, 63, 67, 72,
    91–125
  A Big Jewish Book, 121–22
  "A Personal Manifesto," 100
  "The Poetics of Performance,"
    48–49, 54

Rothenberg, Jerome, and Pierre Joris
    Poems for the Millennium, 148
Rousseau, Jean-Jacques, 64
Rutan, Catherine, 33

Sayre, Henry, 67
    *The Object of Performance: The
        American Avant-Garde Since 1970*,
        70–72
Shelley, Percy, 33
Silliman, Ron, 23, 26, 31, 39, 40, 46,
    52–53, 60, 62, 68, 79, 80, 81–82,
    85–87, 93, 96–97, 136, 147
    "Canons and Institutions: New
        Hope for the Disappeared,"
        64–65
    In the American Tree, 3, 37–46,
        50–52, 54, 67
Simpson, Louis, 6–7, 8, 9, 22, 34
Smith, Dave, 7, 8
    *Local Assays: On Contemporary
        American Poetry*, 10–11, 32
Smith, Dave, and David Bottoms
    *The Morrow Anthology of Younger
        American Poets*, 50–51, 54, 67
Smithson, Robert, 70
Snodgrass, W. D., 16
Snyder, Gary, 48, 95, 96, 120
Socrates, 113
Song, Cathy, 131
Soto, Gary, 76, 130–31
Spicer, Jack, 85
Stafford, William, 9–10
Stein, Gertrude, 27, 45, 46, 66, 68, 95,
    98, 135, 148, 151
Stern, Gerald, 76

Stevens, Wallace, 45, 60, 82, 135
Stitt, Peter, 7, 37
    The World's Hieroglyphic Beauty,
        8–10

Tafolla, Carmen
    "Chicano Literature: Beyond
        Beginnings," 73–74, 76, 77
Thomas, Dylan, 9
Thomas, Lorenzo, 38, 131
Thoreau, Henry David, 23, 115
Tsvetayeva, Marina, 122
Turner, Victor, 100, 108

Vendler, Helen, 7, 33
    *The Harvard Book of Contemporary
        Poetry*, 38, 67
von Hallberg, Robert, 53

Watson, Craig, 40
Watten, Barrett, 23, 40, 62
Wegman, William, 71
Weiner, Hannah, 24, 45
Welch, Lew, 85
Williams, Raymond, 86
Williams, William Carlos, 23, 27, 45,
    66, 68, 135, 139
Williamson, Alan, 7, 24
    *Introspection and Contemporary
        Poetry*, 13–15
Winogrand, Garry, 71
Wordsworth, William, 33
Wright, Charles, 9
Wright, James, 9, 11, 61

Zukofsky, Louis, 45, 68